Prague

SWEDEN

DENMARK

Baltic Sea

GERMANY

Berlin •

POLAND

• PRAGUE

CZECHOSLOVAKIA

HarperCollins*Publishers*

YOUR COLLINS TRAVELLER

Your Collins Traveller Guide will help you find your way around your chosen destination quickly and easily. It is colour-coded for easy reference:

The blue section answers the question 'I would like to see or do something; where do I go and what do I see when I get there?' This section is arranged as an alphabetical list of topics. Within each topic you will find:
- A selection of the best examples on offer.
- How to get there, costs and opening hours for each entry.
- The outstanding features of each entry.
- A simplified map, with each entry plotted and the nearest landmark or transport access.

The red section is a lively and informative gazetteer. It offers:
- Essential facts about the main places and cultural items.
  What is Josefov? Who was Dvořák? Where is Wenceslas Square?
- Practical and invaluable travel information.
  Everything you need to know to help you enjoy yourself and get the most out of your time away, from Accommodation through Boat Trips, Car Hire, Food, Health, Money, Newspapers, Taxis, Telephones to Zoos.

Cross-references:

Type in small capitals - CHURCHES - tells you that more information on an item is available within the topic on churches.

A-Z after an item tells you that more information is available within the gazetteer. Simply look under the appropriate name.

A name in bold - **Prague Castle** - also tells you that more information on an item is available in the gazetteer – again simply look up the name.

CONTENTS

CONTENTS

RED SECTION

INTRODUCTION

Prague shines like a jewel at the very heart of Europe. Like an elegant dowager duchess just awakening after a 50-year enforced slumber, she is dusting herself off and polishing her gems for a new generation of visitors to admire. Prague is without doubt one of Europe's most beautiful and historic cities and, unlike most of her fellow capitals, practically untouched by the ravages of World War II. Prague justly deserves the descriptions of 'the Golden City' and 'the City of a Hundred Spires'.

Scattered over several steep hills and divided by the Vltava (Moldau) river, no other capital in Europe, except Rome, can boast such a complex of historic streets, houses, palaces and churches dating from the Middle Ages onward. Street after street of pastel painted houses and noble dwellings ensure that at virtually every corner the visitor finds something new and exciting to discover. Tiny alleyways, half hidden squares lit by ancient lanterns, magnificent baroque churches and palaces – it is all here tenfold. The war and then 40 years of hardline, lacklustre Communist rule have failed to dim the charm. Everywhere ancient buildings are being restored to their former glory. In between all this splendour lie parks, open spaces and of course, the river.

Modern Prague is a thriving metropolis with an excellent, cheap, rapid-transport system and numerous cafés, nightspots and shops. As for music and culture, you can take your pick from classical concerts and organ recitals to jazz and rock performances held all over the city, and visit museums and galleries galore. The food would bring tears of joy to any returning Austro-Hungarian aristocrat with memories of the good old days. Also worthy of mention is Czech beer; the famous Pilsen and Budweiser can be sampled along with many other, less familiar, but equally delicious local brews. Prague is also fortunate to be surrounded by some spectacular countryside with fantastic castles (such as Konopiště and Karlstein) and forests at every turn, all easily reached on good, uncrowded roads. Bohemia and its capital are destinations that you are unlikely to forget. Among the many visitors who have fallen under their spell are Mozart, Beethoven, Lord Nelson, Galsworthy and Shaw to name but a few.

In many respects the history of the formation of the city accounts for much of its charm. The Prague Basin was first settled in prehistoric

times and of these early inhabitants we know little. They were replaced, around 500 BC, by the Celtic Boii and it was this tribe who gave their name to modern Bohemia. In their turn they were overrun by Slav invaders, the Czechs, sometime in the 4thC AD. They were a pagan and very warlike group who squabbled constantly until a strong leader came on the scene in the shape of Queen Libussa (a sort of Czech Boudicca) with her husband Přemysl. So began the Přemysl dynasty that lasted for almost 500 years. In 873, Prince Bořivoj accepted Christianity and the first foundations of Prague Castle were laid. Christianity had come to the pagan, slavonic Czechs from opposite directions – from Cyril and Methodius (Apostles of the Slavs) from the east and German missionaries from the west – and explains why even today Prague is a meeting place of ideas from east and west.

By the 10thC Prague was a substantial town and a great trading place attracting a large number of German merchants. Strong Germanic influence was to hold sway for the next 900 years and indeed by 1178 there were so many German townsfolk and merchants in the city that a royal

Old Town

decree granted them the same rights as Czech citizens.

When the direct Přemysl line died out in 1306, a strategic, political marriage resulted in the throne being passed to the House of Luxemburg and contacts were made with France and other countries including England, although the main power shift was to the Austro-German camp. It was at this point in history that Bohemia really took the limelight on the Central European stage. Under John of Luxemburg's son, the brilliant Charles IV, Prague was endowed with some of its most famous landmarks, such as the bridge bearing his name, the university and the square known today as Wenceslas Square.

In 1576 the then Holy Roman Emperor, Rudolf II, made Prague the capital of his empire. The city became the leading European centre for art, culture and learning, and the nobility matched this in the construction of magnificent palaces which still, for the most part, exist today. Even though, for the next two centuries, Prague fell under the shadow of Vienna as a provincial outpost, it did not stop the inflow of artists, craftsmen and musicians, ever eager to gain the patronage of some wealthy noble who had a palace there. However, racial differences were always present, with a rivalry between Slav and Teuton which was heightened by the recognition in 1780 of German as the only official language of the

Karlovy Vary

country. Slowly, as the 19thC proceeded, the striving for Czech autonomy from Austria increased. It manifested itself not only in the occasional riot, but also in literature and music (such as that composed by Smetana and Dvořák). New industries grew up and the Czechs and their German-speaking compatriots made Bohemia a seal of quality on glassware and tools. At the turn of the century, Prague saw Europe's most widespread use of the new *Jugendstil* (Art Nouveau) style in architecture. Elegant hotels and cafés vied with those in Vienna and Budapest as the most graceful in the empire.

In 1918, the Austro-Hungarian Empire fell apart and Czechoslovakia emerged as an independent state for the first time in almost 700 years, largely due to the efforts of Tomáš Masaryk. The country was a strange polyglot of Czech, Slovak, Moravian, Hungarian and German. Nevertheless, during the 1920s and '30s the new state was a model democratic country. Hitler ruined all that in 1939 when he invaded Czechoslovakia and after many bitter experiences under the Nazis, the citizens were 'liberated' by the Soviet army in May 1945. The three-and-a-half million German speakers were expelled and there followed 20 years under a dour and hardline left-wing regime. Finally, in the spring of 1968 the population, under the lead of Dubček, revolted. The 'Prague

Karlovy Vary

Spring' rising was put down by the troops of the Warsaw Pact with the utmost severity. However, since 1989 the Communist party no longer dominates the government, and now under the able leadership of playwright Václav Havel, Prague is at last taking her place again as the capital of a democratic sovereign state.

In spite of the turbulent past, Prague has kept its unique architecture and heritage intact. This may not be immediately apparent as you enter through rather grey and uninteresting suburbs. However, once you are in the centre your perceptions will change. Here is the Old Town Square surrounded by stunningly beautiful buildings, the Old Jewish Town, ancient Charles Bridge bedecked with statues, the tiny streets and attractive squares of the Lesser Town, and dominating it all the castle perched high above on its hill. You will need to set aside at least one full day to explore the palaces, the huge St. Vitus' Cathedral, museums and galleries, as well as some wonderful gardens which make up this incredible castle complex. In contrast to the narrow steets and tightly packed buildings of the Old Town is the spacious New Town area located on the other side of the major thoroughfare, Národní třída. Here, the focal point is the enormous Wenceslas Square, a busy area offering cafés, shops and nightlife, surveyed by the equestrian statue of St. Wenceslas, Czechoslovakia's national hero.

As a result of recent events in the country, many changes are taking place in Prague with regard to shops, restaurants, galleries, etc., so be prepared for the unexpected. Whichever of the many attractions you choose to explore and experience, it will not take long for Prague to work its magic on you as it has done on so many before.

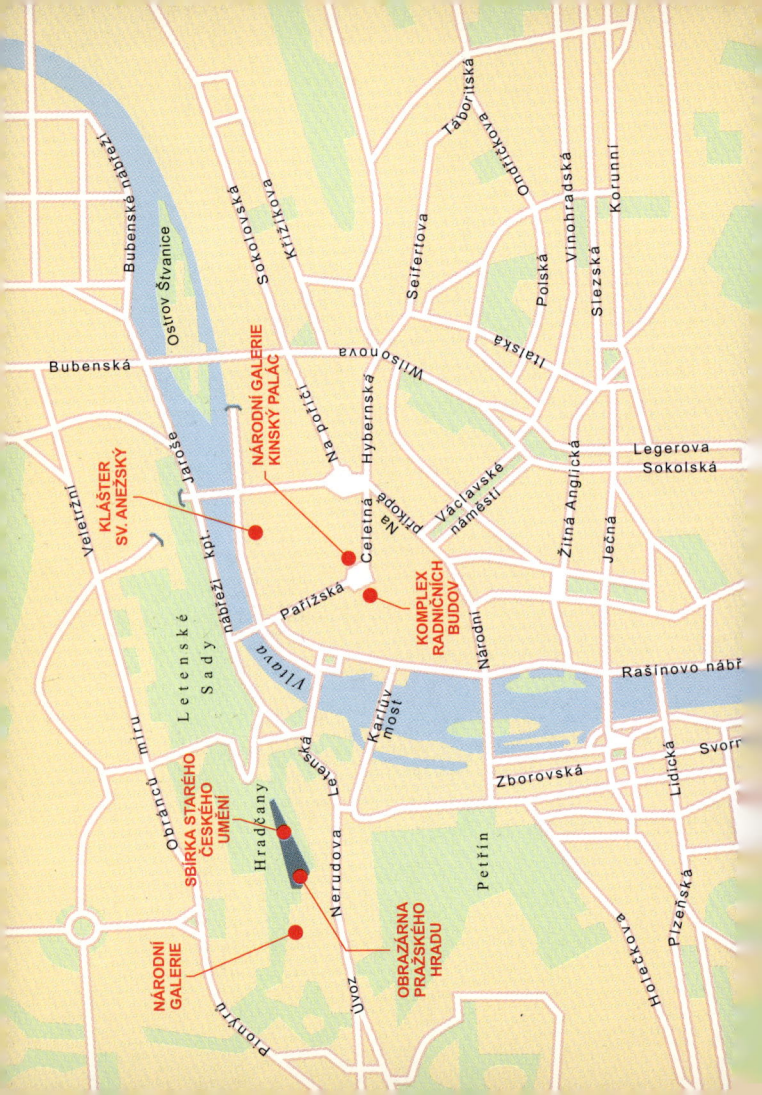

Street and place labels (map):

Bubenské nábřeží
Ostrov Štvanice
Sokolovská
Křižíkova
Táborítská
Ondříčkova
Seifertova
Vinohradská
Korunní
Bubenská
Wilsonova
Polská
Slezská
Italská
NÁRODNÍ GALERIE KINSKÝ PALÁC
Jaroše
Na poříčí
Hybernská
Veletržní
KLÁŠTER SV. ANEŽKY
Celetná
Na příkopě
Václavské náměstí
Legerova
Sokolská
nábřeží kpt.
Pařížská
Žitná
Anglická
Ječná
Letenské Sady
Vltava
KOMPLEX RADNIČNÍCH BUDOV
Národní
Rašínovo nábř.
Obránců míru
Karlův most
Letenská
Zborovská
Lidická
Svorn
SBÍRKA STARÉHO ČESKÉHO UMĚNÍ
Hradčany
Nerudova
Petřín
OBRAŽÁRNA PRAŽSKÉHO HRADU
Pizeňská
Holečkova
NÁRODNÍ GALERIE
Úvoz
Plzeňská

NÁRODNÍ GALERIE (NATIONAL GALLERY) Šternberský Palác, Hradčanské náměstí 15 (side entrance of the Archbishop's Palace).
❏ 1000-1800 Tue.-Sun. Tram 22 to Pohořelec; best by taxi. ❏ Kčs 20.
Superb collection of European masters including Cranach, Tintoretto, Brueghel, Van Dyck, Picasso and many rare works by 19th-20thC artists.

SBÍRKA STARÉHO ČESKÉHO UMĚNÍ (OLD BOHEMIAN COL-LECTION) St. George's Convent, behind St. Vitus' Cathedral, Hradčany.
❏ 1000-1800 Tue.-Sun. Best by taxi. ❏ Kčs 20.
Unique collection of Bohemian art from the 14th-18thC. Sculpture, reliefs, paintings and altarpieces, as well as some very rare Czech icons.

OBRAZÁRNA PRAŽSKÉHO HRADU (CASTLE PICTURE GALLERY) 2nd courtyard, Prague Castle.
❏ 1000-1600. Best by taxi. ❏ Kčs 10.
*Last remnants of the fabulous collection of Rudolf II (see **A-Z**), including Titian, Rubens and Tintoretto. See **PRAGUE CASTLE**.*

KLÁŠTER SV. ANEŽSKÝ (ST. AGNES' CONVENT) Anežská, on the corner of U milosrdných.
❏ 1000-1700 Tue.-Sun. Tram 5, 14, 26; bus 125. ❏ Kčs 20.
*An interesting collection of Czech 19th and 20thC masters. Also has displays of superb porcelain and glassware. See **A-Z**.*

NÁRODNÍ GALERIE KINSKÝ PALÁC (GRAPHICS SECTION) Kinský Palace & U zvonu Tower, Staroměstské náměstí 12.
❏ 1000-1730 Tue.-Sun. Metro Můstek or Staroměstská; tram 17, 18 then walk through Kaprova. ❏ Kčs 10.
Housed in the former palace of the Kinski family; superb drawings, sketches, etc. from all periods. Special visiting exhibitions displayed.

KOMPLEX RADNIČNÍCH BUDOV (OLD TOWN HALL MUNICI-PAL GALLERY) Staroměstské náměstí 1.
❏ 0900-1800. Metro Staroměstská; tram 17, 18. ❏ Kčs 20.
Pictures and sketches associated with Prague.

Bubenské nábřeží

Ostrov Štvanice

Sokolovská

Křižíkova

OBECNÍ DŮM

Táboritská

Ondříčkova

Seifertova

Italská

Wilsonova

Polská

Vinohradská

Korunní

Slezská

Bubenská

Na poříčí

Hybernská

Na příkopě

EUROPA

Legerova

Sokolská

Jaroše

Veletržní

**SNACK BAR
INTERCONTINENTAL
HOTEL**

Celetná

Václavské
náměstí

Žitná

Anglická

Ječná

nábřeží kpt.

Pařížská

**SALON
PAŘÍŽ**

Národní

Vltava

Letenské
Sady

míru

Rašínovo nábř.

Karlův
most

Svorn

Obránců

Letenská

Zborovská

Lidická

Plzeňská

Hradčany

Nerudova

**U ZLATÉ
ULIČKY**

**MALOSTRANSKÁ
KAVÁRNA**

Petřín

**CAFÉ
COLOMBIA**

Úvoz

Holečkova

Plzeňská

Plynojm

EUROPA Václavské náměstí 29 (Wenceslas Sq.).
❏ 0700-2300. Metro Můstek; tram 3, 9, 24. ❏ Moderate.
Old-fashioned café-restaurant under the Europa Hotel with tables outside in summer. There is often a small orchestra performing or a piano being played.

SNACK BAR Intercontinental Hotel, náměstí Curieových.
❏ 0800-2330. Tram 17, 18. ❏ Moderate.
Very American-style coffee shop with lovely views of the river and close to St. Agnes' Convent and the Jewish Town (see **OLD JEWISH TOWN***).*

MALOSTRANSKÁ KAVÁRNA Malostranské náměstí.
❏ 0900-2300. Metro Malostranská & tram 12, 22. ❏ Inexpensive.
In the 1920s and '30s this was the meeting place of artists and intellectuals. Good atmosphere, delicious coffee and cakes.

OBECNÍ DŮM Municipal House, náměstí Republiky.
❏ 0700-2300. Metro Náměstí Republiky; tram 5, 14, 26.
❏ Inexpensive.
Jugendstil *extravaganza in the municipal complex (see* **Municipal House***) facing the square. Excellent coffee and snacks.*

U ZLATÉ ULIČKY Zlatá ulička, within the castle precinct.
❏ 1000-1800. Metro Malostranská then a short walk; tram 18, 22 then up the castle steps (Staré zámecké schody). ❏ Inexpensive.
Provides good coffee and a welcome rest from sightseeing in the castle.

SALON PAŘÍŽ Hotel Paříž, U Obecního domu.
❏ 1000-0100. Metro Náměstí Republiky; tram 5, 14, 26.
❏ Inexpensive.
Serves wonderful Viennese coffee with thick whipped cream.

CAFÉ COLOMBIA Mostecká, Lesser Town side of Charles Bridge.
❏ 0830-2400. Best reached on foot or tram 12, 22 to Malostranské náměstí. ❏ Inexpensive.
Marvellous atmosphere and excellent coffee in cosy surroundings.

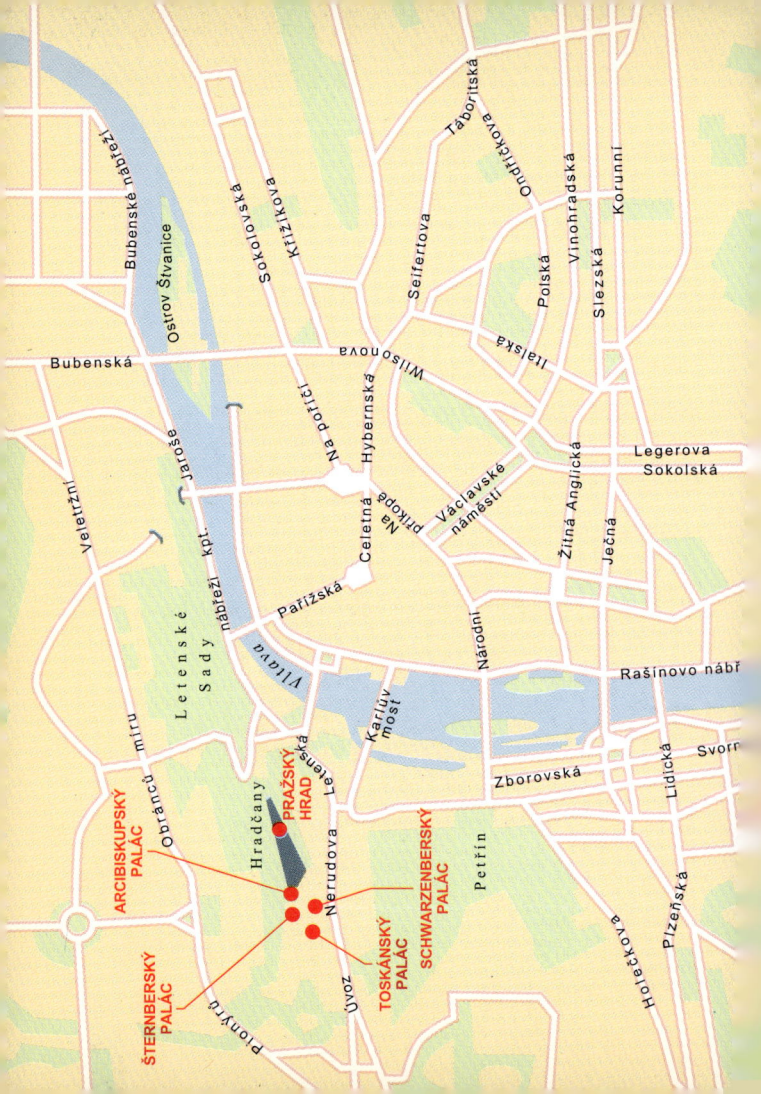

Bubenské nábřeží

Ostrov Štvanice

Sokolovská

Křižíkova

Bubenská

Táboritská

Ondříčkova

Seifertova

Polská

Vinohradská

Slezská

Korunní

Italská

Wilsonova

Na poříčí

Hybernská

Legerova
Sokolská

Veletržní

Jaroše

nábřeží kpt.

Na příkopě

Václavské
náměstí

Žitná Anglická

Ječná

Celetná

Pařížská

Národní

Letenské

Sady

míru

Vltava

Rašínovo nábř

Karlův
most

Lidická

Svorn

Obránců

Letenská

Zborovská

Hradčany

PRAŽSKÝ
HRAD

ARCIBISKUPSKÝ
PALÁC

Nerudova

Petřín

Holečkova

Plzeňská

STERNBERSKÝ
PALÁC

Plzeňská

Úvoz

TOSKÁNSKÝ
PALÁC

SCHWARZENBERSKÝ
PALÁC

CASTLES & PALACES 1

PRAŽSKÝ HRAD (PRAGUE CASTLE) Hradčanské náměstí.
❑ 0900-1600/1700/1800 Tue.-Sun. depending on season; galleries & palaces 1000-1600/1700/1800. Metro Malostranská then up the steps, Staré zámecké schody; tram 12, 22 to Malostranské náměsti or 22 to Pražský Hrad; best by taxi. ❑ Kčs 10 (multi-ticket for galleries & palaces), plus Kčs 5 for certain buildings; cathedral free.
More than a castle, the Hradčany is a whole complex of buildings on a site across the river from the old city centre. See **PRAGUE CASTLE**, **A-Z**.

SCHWARZENBERSKÝ PALÁC (SCHWARZENBERG PALACE)
Hradčanské náměstí.
❑ See above. Access as for the castle (see above). ❑ Kčs 10.
Built 1543-63 for the Lobkowitz family (see **A-Z***) but from 1714 in the hands of the Schwarzenbergs and now the Army Museum (see* **MUSEUMS***). It is the finest example of Bohemian Renaissance style in the city and the wall-painted exterior is unique in Prague.*

TOSKÁNSKÝ PALÁC (TUSCAN PALACE)
Hradčanské náměstí.
❑ Not open to the public. Access as for the castle (see above).
Built in 1695 by the French architect Jean-Baptiste Mathey for the Dukes of Tuscany. It now forms part of the Foreign Ministry and the University.

ARCIBISKUPSKÝ PALÁC (ARCHBISHOP'S PALACE)
Hradčanské náměstí.
❑ Only on Maundy Thu. Access as for the castle (see above).
❑ Free, but an offering is expected.
Seat of the archbishops, built 1550, but constantly extended and altered. Final phase finished in 1764 during the reign of Empress Maria-Theresa.

ŠTERNBERSKÝ PALÁC (STERNBERG PALACE)
Hradčanské náměstí.
❑ 1000-1800 Tue.-Sun. Access as for the castle (see above). ❑ Kčs 20.
Tucked away behind the Archbishop's Palace, the Sternbergs' family seat (built 1700) is now part of the National Gallery (see **ART GALLERIES***). It has a garden which slopes up towards Loreto Church (see* **CHURCHES 1***).*

CASTLES & PALACES 2

BELVEDERE PALACE (also called Letohrádek Královny Anny), Chotkova by Chotkovy Park.
❏ Palace 0900-1700/1800 Tue.-Sun.; gardens 0900-1800 April-Oct. Metro Hradčanská then walk along Ulice K Brusce; tram 18, 22.
❏ Palace Kčs 10, gardens Kčs 5.
Imperial summer palace built 1538-63 in Italian Renaissance style. The magnificent gardens are also worth seeing and contain the 'Singing Fountain' by Francesco Terzia, the Italian sculptor.

VALDŠTEJNSKÝ PALÁC (WALLENSTEIN PALACE)
Valdštejnské náměstí.
❏ Palace closed for restoration; gardens 0830-dusk May-Sep. Metro Malostranská; tram 12, 18, 22 to Letenská. ❏ Free.
First major baroque building in Prague. Albrecht von Wallenstein ordered the demolition of 23 houses to have it constructed by Italian workmen in 1623-30. The garden is a 'must' (see **PARKS & GARDENS***).*

KINSKÝ PALÁC (KINSKÝ PALACE) Staroměstské náměstí.
❏ 1000-1730 Tue.-Sun. Metro Můstek or Staroměstská; tram 17, 18 then walk through Kaprova. ❏ Kčs 10.
Built 1755-65 by Lurago to plans by Kilian Dientzenhofer (see **A-Z***). A German school for 80 years, it now holds the graphics section of the National Gallery (see* **ART GALLERIES***).*

ZÁMEK V TROJI (TROJA PALACE) U trojského zámku, Troja, Prague 7.
❏ 1000-1700 Tue.-Sun.; Sat. only in winter. Special bus 112. ❏ Kčs 10.
Magnificent baroque palace in a pleasant setting in the city outskirts. The gardens are lovely in summer. Combine with a visit to the zoo (see **CHILDREN**, **Zoological Gardens***).*

HRAD KARLŠTEJN (KARLSTEIN CASTLE) Karlštejn.
❏ 1000-1500 Tue.-Sun. (Mar.-April), 0900-1700 (May-Sep.), 1000-1600 (Oct.-Dec.). Off the Plzeň-Prague motorway or main route 4. ❏ Kčs 60.
Built by Charles IV (see **A-Z***) to house the crown jewels. The turreted castle sits in an impressive hill-top location. See* **EXCURSION 2***.*

NÁRODNÍ TECHNICKÉ MUZEUM
ZOOLOGICKÁ ZAHRADA PRAHA
ASTRONOMICAL CLOCK
KARLŮV MOST
HORSE & CARRIAGE RIDE
FUNICULAR RAILWAY
LATERNA MAGICA
Veletržní
Bubenská
Bubenské nábřeží
Ostrov Štvanice
Obránců míru
Letenské Sady
Jaroše
nábřeží kpt.
Pionýrů
Hradčany
Vltava
Sokolovská
Křižíkova
Pařížská
Letenská
Nerudova
Úvoz
Na poříčí
Celetná
Hybernská
Na příkopě
Wilsonova
Seifertova
Táboritská
Václavské náměstí
Petřín
Národní
Ondříčkova
Italská
Polská
Zborovská
Žitná Anglická
Vinohradská
Slezská
Ječná
Korunní
Holečkova
Rašínovo nábře
Sokolská
Legerova
Plzeňská
Lidická
Svorno

HORSE & CARRIAGE RIDE Staroměstské náměstí, outside the Old Town Hall.
❏ No fixed dep. times, await return of coaches. Metro Staroměstská; tram 17, 18 then walk through Kaprova. ❏ Kčs 300-400.
*A 1-hr drive around the Old Town (see **A-Z**) or further afield.*

ASTRONOMICAL CLOCK Outside the Old Town Hall.
❏ 24 hr. Metro Staroměstská; tram 17, 18. ❏ Free.
*One of the wonders of Prague and a fascinating sight. See **A-Z**.*

ZOOLOGICKÁ ZAHRADA PRAHA (PRAGUE ZOO)
U trojského zámku, Troja, Prague 7.
❏ 0900-1 hr before dusk. Special bus 112. ❏ Kčs 10.
*Excellent zoo in attractive surroundings next to Troja Palace (see **CASTLES & PALACES 2**). See **Zoological Gardens**.*

NÁRODNÍ TECHNICKÉ MUZEUM Kostelní 42.
❏ 0900-1700 Tue.-Sun. Tram 1, 8, 25, 26; bus 125. ❏ Kčs 10, child 5.
*Technical museum with plenty of interest for children. See **MUSEUMS**.*

KARLŮV MOST (CHARLES BRIDGE) From Křižovnické náměstí. Tram 17, 18.
*Children and adults will enjoy the magnificent panorama from the bridge up to the Castle Hill. Boat trips are available in summer. See **A-Z**.*

LATERNA MAGICA (THE MAGIC LANTERN) Nová scéna Theatre, Národní 4.
❏ Daily, check performance times with hotel reception or tel: 206260. Metro Můstek or Národní třída; tram 9, 18, 21, 22. ❏ Prices vary.
*Unique to Prague, this 'Magic Circus' with shadow puppets, etc. has shows for adults (performance 2000) as well as for children. See **WALK 2**.*

FUNICULAR RAILWAY U lanové dráhy, off Újezd.
❏ 0500-2400. Tram 12, 22. ❏ Kčs 4.
*A ride up this exciting railway will take you to the top of the huge Petřín park (see **PARKS & GARDENS**) overlooking the city.*

Bubenské nábřeží
Sokolovská
Křižíkova
Táboritská
Ondříčkova
Seifertova
Vinohradská
Korunní
Polská
Slezská
Italská

Ostrov Štvanice
Bubenská
Wilsonova
Na poříčí
Hybernská
Na příkopě
Václavské náměstí
Legerova
Sokolská

Jaroše
Žitná
Anglická
Ječná

Veletržní
nábřeží kpt.
KOSTEL
PANNY MARIE
PŘED TÝNEM
Celetná
Pařížská

Letenské Sady
Vltava
Národní
Rašínovo nábř.

Obránců míru
Karlův most
Zborovská
Lidická
Svorn

SVATÝ JIŘÍ
Hradčany
Letenská
CHRÁM SVATÉHO MIKULÁŠE
Petřín
Plzeňská
Holečkova

Nerudova
SVATÝ VÍT
LORETA
Úvoz
Pionýrů

❑ 0900-1800. ❑ Free, unless stated otherwise.

SVATÝ VÍT (ST. VITUS' CATHEDRAL) Prague Castle.
❑ 0900-1600/1700/1800 depending on season. Metro Hradčanská then walk uphill; tram 22 to Pražský Hrad; best by taxi.
This enormous Gothic church was built 1344-1929. Climb the 96 m-high tower for magnificent views of the city. See **St. Vitus' Cathedral**.

SVATÝ JIŘÍ (ST. GEORGE'S BASILICA) Prague Castle.
❑ 0900-1600/1700/1800 depending on season. Metro Hradčanská then walk uphill; tram 22 to Pražský Hrad; best by taxi. ❑ Kčs 4.
Oldest Romanesque church in Prague, built in 920 but redecorated and refurbished in 1120. Totally different in style from all others it contains several remnants of very early wall paintings. See **PRAGUE CASTLE**.

CHRÁM SVATÉHO MIKULÁŠE (ST. NICHOLAS' CHURCH IN THE LESSER TOWN) Malostranské náměstí.
Metro Malostranská; tram 12, 22.
The largest and most impressive baroque church in Prague was built (1704-52) for the Jesuits by the Dientzenhofers (see **A-Z**). *A massive 1500 sq. m ceiling fresco depicts the life of St. Nicholas. See* **A-Z**.

LORETA (OUR LADY OF LORETO) Loretánské náměstí.
Tram 22, 23 to Pohořelec.
Monastery church and pilgrimage centre on account of the copy of the Santa Casa of Loreto in Italy. The treasury with monstrance containing 6200 diamonds should not be missed. See **MUSTS**, **Our Lady of Loreto**.

KOSTEL PANNY MARIE PŘED TÝNEM (ST. MARY BEFORE TÝN) Staroměstské náměstí.
Metro Staroměstská; tram 17, 18 and walk through Kaprova.
The strangely decorated spires of this church are one of Prague's best-known landmarks. Built in 1365 in front of the Týn (customs) yard with the towers added in 1511, and redecorated in the 17thC. It contains the oldest font in the city (1414) and the tomb of Danish astronomer Tycho Brahe (1546-1601). Currently being restored; enter by the south porch.

KOSTEL SVATÉHO JANA NEPOMUCKÉHO NA SKALCE

CHRÁM SVATÉHO JAKUBA

KOSTEL PANNY MARIE SNĚŽNÉ

KOSTEL SVATÉHO MIKULÁŠE

ROTUNDA SVATÉHO MARTINA

Bubenské nábřeží

Sokolovská

Křižíkova

Ostrov Štvanice

Bubenská

Na poříčí

Jaroše

Wilsonova

Hybernská

Seifertova

Táboritská

Oldřichova

Vinohradská

Polská

Slezská

Korunní

Italská

Legerova

Sokolská

Na příkopě

Václavské náměstí

Celetná

Pařížská

nábřeží kpt.

Veletržní

Letenské Sady

Vltava

Obránců míru

Letenská

Nerudova

Hradčany

Petřín

Úvoz

Pionýrů

Karlův most

Národní

Žitná

Anglická

Ječná

Zborovská

Zborovská

Lidická

Svorno...

Rašínovo nábře...

Holečkova

Plzeňská

CHRÁM SVATÉHO JAKUBA (CHURCH OF ST. JACOB/ST. JAMES) Jakubská.
Metro Náměstí Republiky; tram 5, 14, 26 to Revoluční.
Impressive baroque interior, completed 1689-1702. Magnificent decoration and interesting tombs. Organ recitals and sung Mass with an orchestra at 1100 on Sun.

KOSTEL SVATÉHO MIKULÁŠE (ST. NICHOLAS' CHURCH IN THE OLD TOWN) Staroměstské náměstí.
Metro Staroměstská; tram 17, 18 and walk through Kaprova.
Not to be confused with the church of the same name in the Lesser Town (see **CHURCHES 1***), this elegant white church with its twin towers was built in 1732. It was once the Russian Orthodox church (1870-1914) and houses one of the biggest crystal chandeliers ever made in Bohemia. Mozart (see* **A-Z***), who lived next door, was a parishioner.*

KOSTEL PANNY MARIE SNĚŽNÉ (ST. MARY OF THE SNOWS) Jungmannovo náměstí.
Metro Můstek; tram 6, 9, 18, 21, 22 to Národní.
Hidden behind Wenceslas Sq. (see **A-Z***) this is Prague's tallest Gothic church (35 m high), of which only part remains. It contains the city's largest altarpiece.*

ROTUNDA SVATÉHO MARTINA (ST. MARTIN-IN-THE-CHAPEL) On Vyšehrad Hill.
Metro Vyšehrad; tram 7, 18, 24 to Vyšehrad.
One of only three remaining round churches in Prague, dating from the 11thC. Close by is SS Peter and Paul's Victorian Gothic pile and from the hill there are magnificent views over the river. See **Vyšehrad***.*

KOSTEL SVATÉHO JANA NEPOMUCKÉHO NA SKALCE (CHURCH OF ST. JOHN NEPOMUK ON THE CLIFF)
Vyšehradská, opposite Na Slovanech Monastery.
Tram 18, 24.
Unusually sited baroque church by Kilian Dientzenhofer (see **A-Z***), built in 1730. It has a superbly painted inner dome. See* **Nepomuk***.*

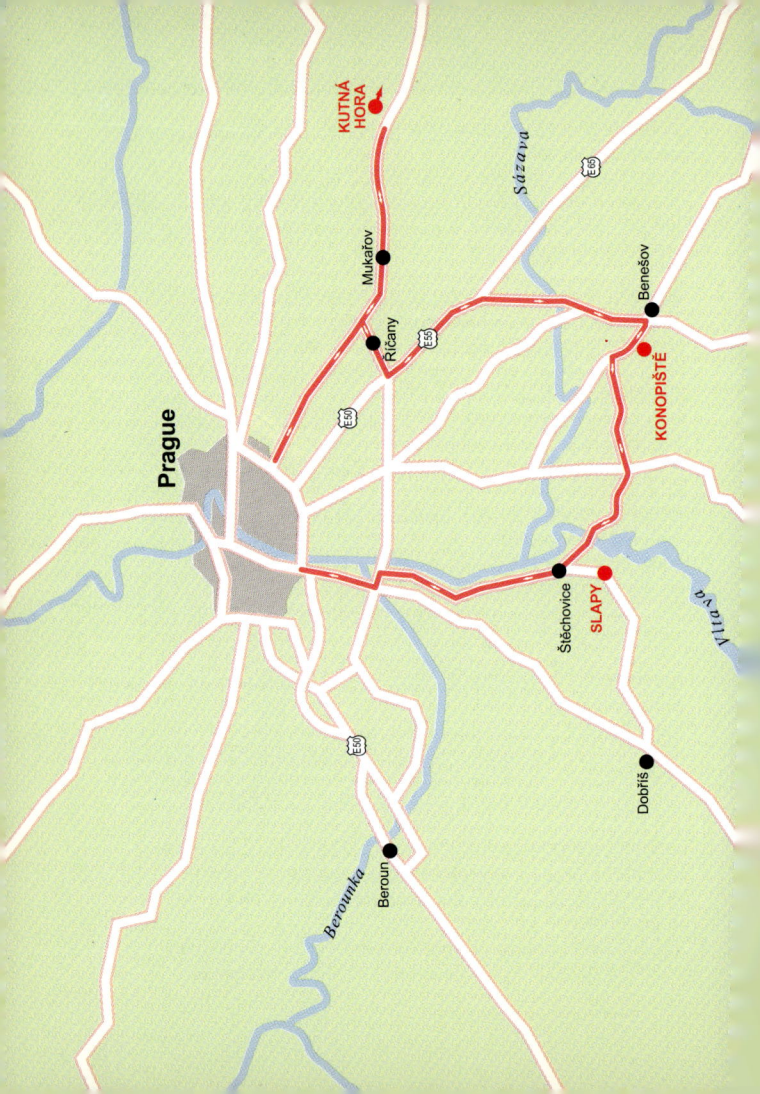

KUTNÁ HORA

Sázava

E65

Mukařov

Benešov

Říčany

E55

KONOPIŠTĚ

E50

Prague

Štěchovice

SLAPY

E50

Dobříš

Vltava

Berounka

Beroun

*Half- or full-day excursion to the attractive district of Jevany, the castle at Konopiště (see **A-Z**) and the Vltava lakes.*

Leave Prague on the Kutná Hora road and follow it for 13 km until you reach the charming small settlement of Jevany which is strung out along the main road near a series of small lakes and ponds with wooded surroundings. If you wish to make this a full-day's outing, continue on this road until you reach Kutná Hora (see **A-Z**), the ancient silver-mining centre and site of the magnificent cathedral of St. Barbara, patron saint of miners. There are many pretty streets to explore in the town. Otherwise, take the turn-off for Říčany and join the main motorway E 50/55/65 heading towards Brno and Bratislava. Approximately 28 km from Prague take the exit to Benešov and Tábor. The main road bypasses Benešov and on that bypass you will see to your right the signpost for Konopiště which is 2 km away. Park up in the area in front of the Hotel Nová Myslivna and crossing the main road follow a very steep, wooded path which will bring you out at the entrance to the castle where you can see bears in a pit and numerous peacocks strutting around. The castle is open 0900-1700 Tue.-Sun., closed Nov., Mar., and on days following a public hol.; Kčs 120. From Konopiště follow the road indicated to Slapy. For the first 900 m drive slowly and look to your left where you have splendid views over the lake to the castle above. Drive on via Vyhlidka where the road climbs and there are magnificent views over the lakes created by the damming of the Vltava river (see **A-Z**). This is a dead-end road as traffic can no longer approach Slapy across the dam. However, at the end of the panoramic drive is the tiny settlement of Nová Rabyně with a good restaurant, lovely views and boat trips in summer. Now return along the same road for approximately 6 km until you reach a crossroads. Turn left and carry on through beautiful countryside via Vysoký Újezd and Krňany to Štěchovice. The main road will carry you over a bridge to bring you to the other side of the Vltava where you should turn immediately right. It is not very well signposted to Prague (Praha). The journey back to the city is very attractive as it follows the river the whole way and eventually brings you back to the embankment just by the Intercontinental Hotel in the centre of Prague without having to negotiate the suburbs. (Total 190 km.)

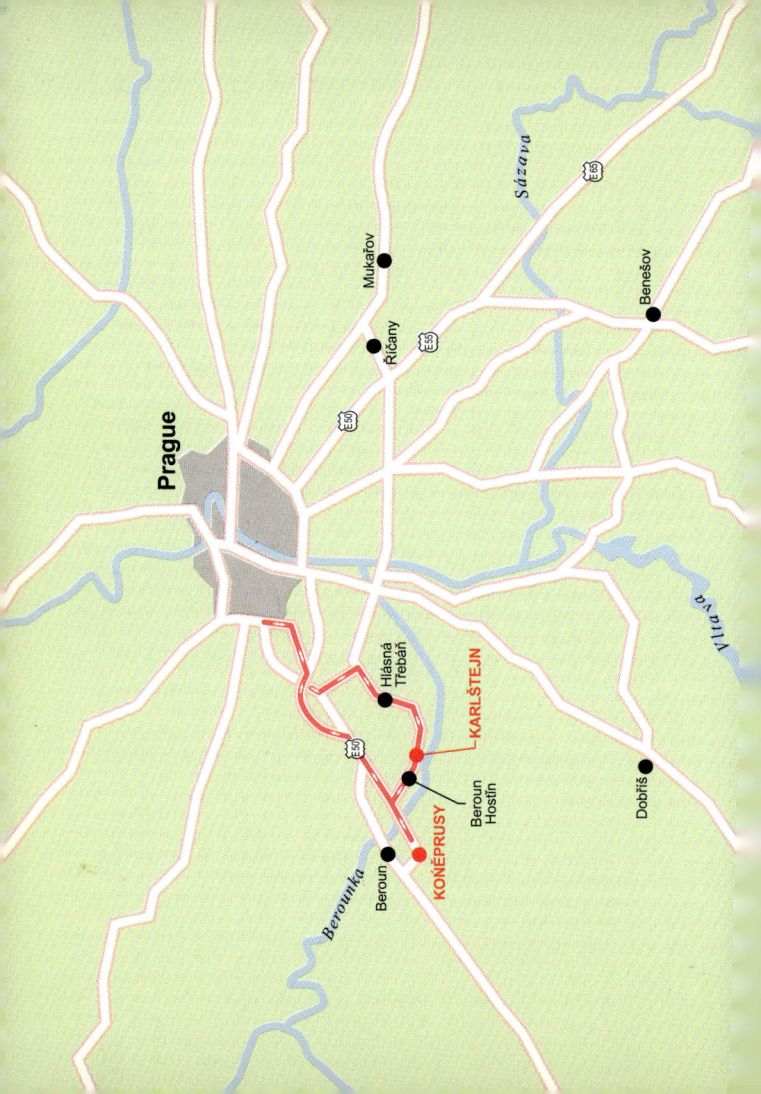

Prague

Sázava

E55

Mukařov

Benešov

Říčany

E55

E55

Hlásná
Třebaň

KARLŠTEJN

E50

Beroun
Hostín

Vltava

Dobříš

KONĚPRUSY

Beroun

Berounka

Karlštejn Castle

*Half- or full-day excursion to the dramatic Karlštejn Castle (see **A-Z**) and surrounding countryside.*

Leave Prague on the Plzeň motorway (E 50/D 5) marked Pilsen-Nürnberg in blue. In about 25 km you will see a sign for Karlštejn (Karlstein) and Loděnice. Follow the road round a quarry and upward into lovely countryside until you reach the village of Hlásná Třebáň where you will find a T-junction with the turn-off for Karlštejn unexpect-edly to the right (badly signposted). If you wish to explore the lovely area along the banks of the Berounka river (which offers good picnic and swimming opportunities) before visiting the castle, turn left through Hlásná Třebáň and drive for about 1 km. Otherwise, head for Karlštejn as indicated. The castle is hidden from the road and the car park, on the left by a snack bar, is easy to miss. If you see a small iron bridge on the left, you have come too far. From the car park walk through the village which is to the right of the road (note that parking in the village is for residents only). The castle is 1.5 km from the car park and uphill so good walking shoes will be needed. As you approach you will see what looks like a scene from Transylvania unfold as the turreted castle comes into view. The tour of the castle takes 1 hr and it should not be missed (see **CASTLES & PALACES 2**). The highlight is the Chapel of the Cross, bedecked in semiprecious stones such as amber and jade. If you want refreshments after visiting the castle, take the car over the little iron bridge and go to the Hotel Mlýn on the opposite bank from where there are lovely views over the water meadows and the river.
If you wish, you can carry on to Koněprusy (11 km away, follow the sign-posts) and see the magnificent caves (0900-1600 April-Oct.; Kčs 15). Otherwise, carry on along the main road on the castle side of the river towards Beroun. The scenery is really quite outstanding and in parts is almost alpine. Pass through Beroun Hostín and so onto the outskirts of the rather grim industrial town of Beroun. You do not need to enter the town as the road passes underneath the Plzeň-Prague motorway and links with it after about 3 km for your return journey. There is a filling sta-tion (with lead-free petrol) on the approach to the motorway. Once in the Prague suburbs look for signs which read 'Centrum' to return you to the city centre. (Total 100 km.)

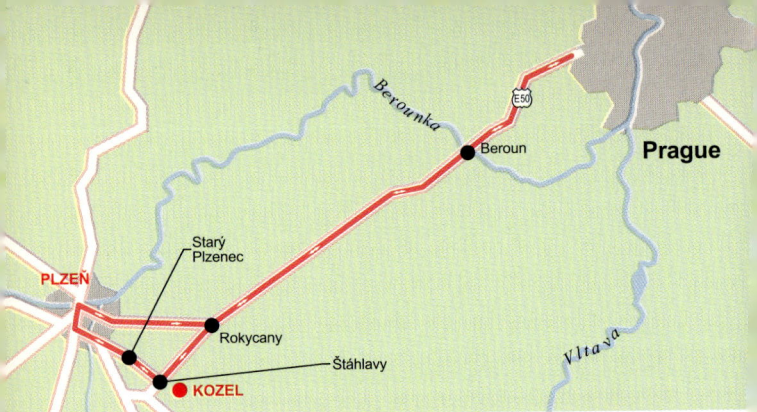

Berounka

E50

Beroun

Prague

Starý
Plzenec

PLZEŇ

Rokycany

Štáhlavy

KOZEL

Vltava

PLZEŇ

Sady 5. května

Veleslavínova

BREWERY
MUSEUM

Solní

Pražská

náměstí
Republiky

Tyršova

ST. BARTHOLOMEW'S
CHURCH

Radbuza

Prešovská

Zbrojnická

Františkánská

Hotel
Continental

P

To Prague

PILSENER
URQUELL
BREWERY

Smetanovy sady

Kopeckého sady

Chodkovské nábřeží

Denisovo nábřeží

WEST BOHEMIAN
MUSEUM

Moskevská

Moskevská

Mikulášská

To Kozel

A one-day trip to a beautiful hunting lodge and the famous brewing town.

Leave Prague on the Plzeň motorway (E 50/D 5). At Rokycany, 30 km from Plzeň, follow the main road through the town until you see a road to your left indicating Šťáhlavy – this is just before you leave the munici- pal limits sign (the name Rokycany with a diagonal line through it). You then have a pretty drive through typical forested Bohemian countryside as you head towards the village of Šťáhlavy. Just before the bridge on the edge of town, you will see on your left a small lane which is unsign- posted. Turn up the lane and follow it past several small houses until it enters deep forest. After about 1.5 km, you will see to your right a leafy track and a white gate. Park the car and enter. This is the rear entrance to the delightful hunting lodge and summer residence of Kozel, built in the 18thC in typical Bohemian style. The pastel-coloured interior is absolutely spellbinding. There is also a splendid collection of armour, magnificent 18thC Meissen porcelain and wonderful gardens with views over Šťáhlavy and beyond (1000-1200, 1300-1700 summer; Kčs 15). Return down the lane to Šťáhlavy to visit a most unusual church, designed by Czernin, and then continue for 1 km along the Plzeň road to see his baroque memorial chapel (on the left). Continue to Starý Plzenec (Little Pilsen) and enter Plzeň (see **A-Z**) under the rail bridge near the main station. Park up near the massive, turn-of-the-century Hotel Continental and the West Bohemian Museum. At the end of the green square you will see a row of tiny, white-painted gabled houses. These are butcher shops from the Middle Ages, now an exhibition cen- tre. Follow the tram tracks into the main square and visit St. Bartholomew's Church and the impressive town hall. It is one of the largest town squares of its type in Europe and there are several good restaurants and bars here. Now cross over to the Brewery Museum in Veleslavínova (0900-1700 Tue.-Sun.; Kčs 10). If you want to taste the real thing then follow the Prague signs out of the town. On your left is the vast expanse of the Pilsener Urquell Brewery (Prazdroj). Ask at the ornate gatehouse for tour details, they are usually every hour and free. Drivers remember to avoid the alcohol as the penalties if you are caught are very severe. Return to Prague by the main road through Rokycany and Beroun, then join the motorway. (Total 200 km.)

MUZEUM HLAVNÍHO MĚSTA PRAHY

MUZEUM ANTONÍNA DVOŘÁKA

NÁRODNÍ TECHNICKÉ MUZEUM

UMĚLECKOPRŮMYSLOVÉ MUZEUM

SMETANOVO MUZEUM

VOJENSKÉ MUZEUM

Bubenské nábřeží

Ostrov Štvanice

Sokolovská

Křižíkova

Bubenská

Na poříčí

Wilsonova

Seifertova

Táboritská

Ondříčkova

Vinohradská

Korunní

Polská

Slezská

Italská

Hybernská

Legerova
Sokolská

Žitná

Anglická

Ječná

Celetná

Na příkopě

Václavské náměstí

Národní

Pařížská

Karlův most

Rašínovo nábř

Veletržní

Jaroše

kpt.

nábřeží

Vltava

Letenská

Zborovská

Svorn

Lidická

Letenské Sady

Obránců míru

Hradčany

Nerudova

Úvoz

Petřín

Plzeňská

Holečkova

Pionýrů

MUZEUM HLAVNÍHO MĚSTA PRAHY (MUSEUM OF THE CITY OF PRAGUE) End of Na poříčí in Švermovy sady park.
❏ 1000-1230, 1330-1800 Tue.-Sun. Metro Sokolovská/Florenc; tram 3, 8, 24. ❏ Kčs 10.
The history of the city from the earliest times including relics from houses now demolished and a model of Prague as it was in the early 19thC.

UMĚLECKOPRŮMYSLOVÉ MUZEUM (MUSEUM OF APPLIED ARTS) 17. listopadu 2.
❏ 1000-1800 Tue.-Sun. Metro Staroměstská; tram 17, 18. ❏ Kčs 12.
Czech and other European arts and crafts, as well as a magnificent display of porcelain, drinking cups and Bohemian glass.

NÁRODNÍ TECHNICKÉ MUZEUM (NATIONAL TECHNICAL MUSEUM) Kostelní 42.
❏ 0900-1700 Tue.-Sun. Metro Hradčanská or Vltavská then tram 1, 8, 25, 26 to Letenské náměstí; bus 125. ❏ Kčs 10, child 5.
Excellent display of all manner of transport, astronomical equipment and household items related to Czechoslovakia. See **CHILDREN**.

MUZEUM ANTONÍNA DVOŘÁKA (ANTONÍN DVOŘÁK MUSEUM) Villa Amerika, Ke Karlovu 2.
❏ 1000-1700 Tue.-Sun. Metro I. P. Pavlova; tram 4, 6, 16, 22; bus 148, 272. ❏ Kčs 10.
Collection of items associated with the Czech composer (see **Dvořák***).*

VOJENSKÉ MUZEUM (CZECH ARMY MUSEUM)
Schwarzenberský Palác, Hradčanské náměstí.
❏ 1000-1800 Tue.-Sun. For access see **PRAGUE CASTLE**. ❏ Kčs 10.
One of the finest military museums in the world. See **PRAGUE CASTLE**.

SMETANOVO MUZEUM (SMETANA MUSEUM) Novotného lávka.
❏ 1000-1700 Wed.-Mon. Tram 17, 18. ❏ Kčs 4.
A display of items associated with Bedřich Smetana (see **A-Z***). His composition* Vltava *plays in the background while you have views of the river (see* **Vltava***) itself and Charles Bridge (see* **A-Z***) from the windows.*

Bubenské nábřeží

Bubenská

Ostrov Štvanice

Sokolovská

Křižíkova

Jaroše

Veletržní

Letenské Sady

nábřeží kpt.

Obránců míru

Vltava

Letenská

Hradčany

Nerudova

Úvoz

Plzeňská

Táboritská

Ondříčkova

Vinohradská

Slezská

Korunní

Seifertova

Wilsonova

Na poříčí

Hybernská

Na příkopě

Celetná

Pařížská

Polská

Italská

Žitná

Anglická

Ječná

Legerova

Sokolská

Národní

Rašínovo nábře

Zborovská

Svorno

Lidická

Petřín

Holečkova

Pelřínská

STAROMĚSTSKÉ NÁMĚSTÍ

KARLŮV MOST

VÁCLAVSKÉ NÁMĚSTÍ

PRAŽSKÝ HRAD

VALDŠTEJNSKÁ ZAHRADA

LORETA

STAROMĚSTSKÉ NÁMĚSTÍ (OLD TOWN SQUARE)
Metro Staroměstská; tram 17, 18 then walk up Kaprova or 5, 14, 26 to náměstí Republiky and walk down Celetná under the Powder Tower (see **A-Z**).
*One of the finest and best-preserved medieval squares in Europe, surrounded by superb buildings, churches, and the interesting little streets of the Old Town (see **A-Z**). The Old Town Hall (see **A-Z**) and Astronomical Clock (see **A-Z**) are also located in the square.*

KARLŮV MOST (CHARLES BRIDGE)
Metro Staroměstská; tram 17, 18 to Křižovnická.
*Ancient bridge, bedecked by statues, crossing the Vltava river. See **A-Z**.*

VÁCLAVSKÉ NÁMĚSTÍ (WENCESLAS SQUARE)
Metro Můstek or Muzeum; tram 3, 9, 14, 24.
*Centre of modern Prague, dominated by a statue of Wenceslas. See **A-Z**.*

PRAŽSKÝ HRAD (PRAGUE CASTLE) Hradčany.
Metro Malostranská then walk uphill by the steps, Staré zámeké schody; tram 12, 18, 22 to Malostranské náměstí then walk up the hill or tram 22 to Pražský Hrad; best by taxi.
Entire complex of palaces, convents, galleries and the famous St. Vitus' Cathedral (see CHURCHES 1*), resting place of St. Wenceslas. Fabulous views over the city. See* CASTLES & PALACES 1*,* PRAGUE CASTLE*.*

LORETA (OUR LADY OF LORETO) Loretánské náměstí.
Tram 22, 23 to Pohořelec.
The church contains a treasury of fabulous articles (in the Loretánský klášter). The walk back down Úvoz and Nerudova streets gives a good impression of Old Prague. See CHURCHES 1*,* PRAGUE CASTLE*,* **Our Lady of Loreto***.*

VALDŠTEJNSKÁ ZAHRADA (WALLENSTEIN PALACE GARDENS) Letenská. Metro Malostranská; tram 12, 18, 22.
Gorgeous formal garden with loggia-protected terrace, bedecked by statues, sitting at the foot of Prague Castle (see **A-Z***). See* PARKS & GARDENS*.*

Map labels:

- Bubenské nábřeží
- Ostrov Štvanice
- Sokolovská
- Křižíkova
- Taboritská
- Ondříčkova
- Seifertova
- Polská
- Vinohradská
- Slezská
- Korunní
- Bubenská
- Wilsonova
- Italská
- HOTEL FORUM CASINO
- PARK CLUB
- Veletržní
- Jaroše
- Na poříčí
- Hybernská
- EST-BAR
- Legerova
- Sokolská
- CASCADE BAR
- Na příkopě
- Václavské náměstí
- PRAGA
- Žitná
- Anglická
- Ječná
- Celetná
- ALHAMBRA
- Pařížská
- VIOLA
- Letenské Sady
- nábřeží kpt.
- Vltava
- Rašínovo nábře
- Karlův most
- REDUTA
- Národní
- Obránců miru
- Letenská
- Svornc
- Hradčany
- Nerudova
- Zborovská
- Lidická
- Úvoz
- Petřín
- Plzeňská
- Holečkova
- Plonýřa

EST-BAR Hotel Esplanade, Washingtonova 19.
❏ 1900-0200 Mon.-Sat. Metro Muzeum; tram 3, 9, 11, 24. ❏ Moderate.
Traditional restaurant with live music, situated in this early-20thC hotel.

ALHAMBRA Václavské náměstí 5.
❏ 2030 till late. Metro Můstek; tram 3, 9, 24. ❏ Moderate.
Prague's best-known variety/cabaret show. Dancing, drinks, etc. plus show. Best booked through your hotel porter.

PRAGA Vodičkova 30.
❏ 2000 till late Tue.-Sun. Metro Národní třída then walk up Jungmannova; tram 3, 9, 24. ❏ Moderate.
International variety programme and dancing. Book through hotel porter.

REDUTA Národní 20.
❏ 2100 till late Mon.-Sat. Metro Národní třída; tram 9, 18, 21, 22.
❏ Moderate.
Prague's best-known jazz club. Book through your hotel.

CASCADE BAR Rybná 8.
❏ 2100 till late. Metro Náměstí Republiky; tram 3, 14, 26.
❏ Moderate.
*Good, lively nightspot on the outskirts of the Old Town (see **A-Z**).*

PARK CLUB Veletržní 20.
❏ Early afternoon onward. Tram 5, 12, 17. ❏ Moderate.
Smart, elegant club attached to the Park Hotel. Good service.

VIOLA Národní 7.
❏ 1830 till late. Metro Můstek; tram 6, 9, 18, 21, 22. ❏ Moderate.
*Strange but fascinating mixture of songs, poetry, jazz and chamber music in a convivial atmosphere (see **RESTAURANTS 1**).*

HOTEL FORUM CASINO Hotel Forum, Kongresová.
❏ 1800-0400. Metro Vyšehrad. ❏ Free.
Smart new casino for roulette, blackjack, etc. Play in US$.

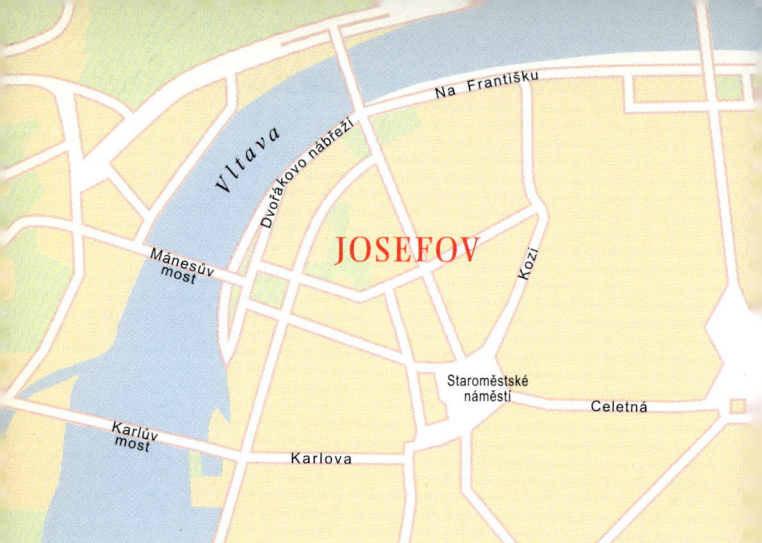

Vltava

Na Františku

Dvořákovo nábřeží

JOSEFOV

Kozí

Mánesův most

Staroměstské náměstí

Celetná

Karlův most

Karlova

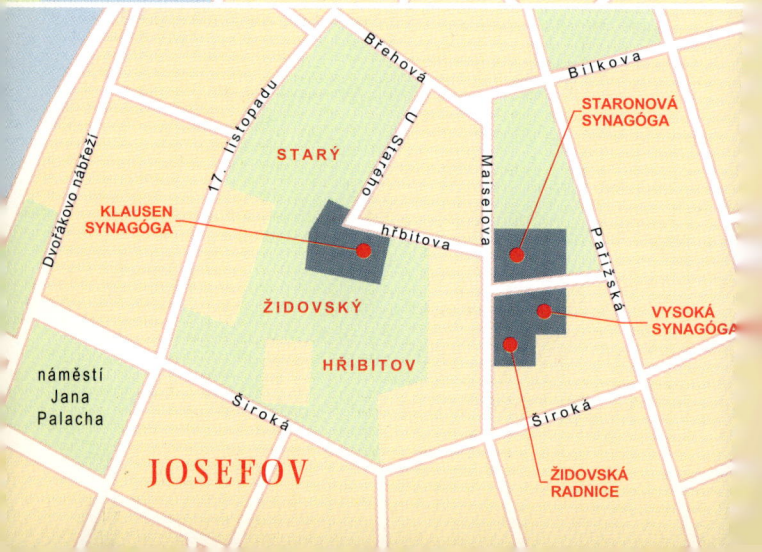

Břehová

Bílkova

Dvořákovo nábřeží

17. listopadu

U Starého

STARÝ

Maiselova

STARONOVÁ SYNAGÓGA

Pařížská

KLAUSEN SYNAGÓGA

hřbitova

ŽIDOVSKÝ

VYSOKÁ SYNAGÓGA

náměstí Jana Palacha

HŘBITOV

Široká

Široká

JOSEFOV

ŽIDOVSKÁ RADNICE

Located just to the west of Pařížská near the Intercontinental Hotel in the Old Town (see **A-Z**). ❏ All the monuments are open 0900-1700, till 1630 in winter. The synagogues are open daily except Sat. and Jewish hol. (headcovering needed). Metro Staroměstská; tram 17, 18 to Čechův most. See **Josefov**.

STARONOVÁ SYNAGÓGA (OLD-NEW SYNAGOGUE)
The oldest synagogue still in use in Europe, it was built in 1270 in the style of a Cistercian chapel. The flag inside was given by Kaiser Ferdinand for the Jews' loyalty during the Swedish occupation in 1648. The name of the synagogue is confusing because it is in the 'Old Town'.

ŽIDOVSKÁ RADNICE (JEWISH TOWN HALL)
The seat of the Chief Rabbi and home to an excellent kosher restaurant. Note the interesting clock tower (1763), showing standard Prague time with another face below, in Hebrew, with the hands going backwards.

VYSOKÁ SYNAGÓGA (HIGH SYNAGOGUE/TOWN HALL SYN-AGOGUE)
❏ Museum 0900-1700, till 1630 in winter. ❏ Kčs 5.
Forms part of the State Jewish Museum and contains dozens of artefacts from all over Bohemia. The ticket allows entry to all places of interest including the cemetery. There is a catalogue in English, priced Kčs 3.80.

KLAUSEN SYNAGÓGA (KLAUSEN SYNAGOGUE)
An exhibition of Jewish daily life as well as a very interesting collection of photographs of ghetto life all over Europe housed in a place of worship dating from 1689.

STARÝ ŽIDOVSKÝ HŘIBITOV (OLD JEWISH CEMETERY)
One of the most important sights in the Old Jewish Town, the oldest grave-stone is dated 1439, the latest 1787. Over 200,000 souls are buried under a forest of upright stones. See the grave of Rabbi Löw (d. 1609) who invented the artificial man, or robot (a Czech word meaning 'worker'), known as the Golem which was a forerunner of Frankenstein.

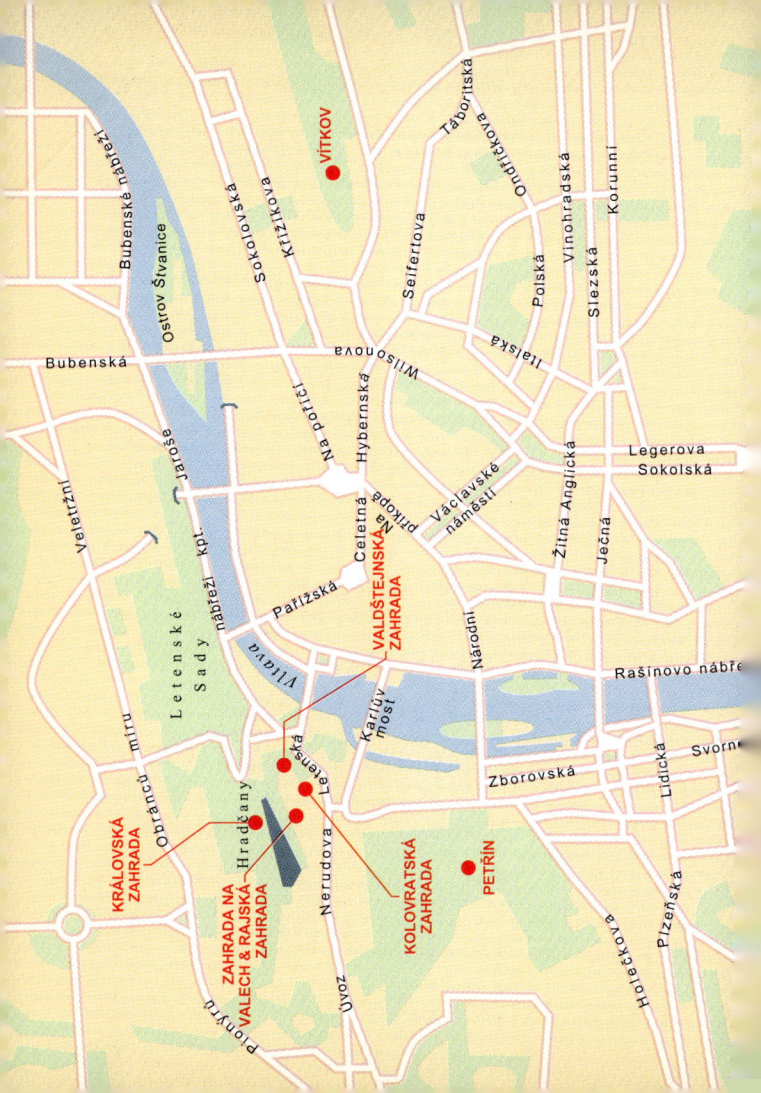

Bubenské nábřeží
VÍTKOV
Ostrov Štvanice
Sokolovská
Křižíkova
Táboritská
Ondříčkova
Vinohradská
Korunní
Seifertova
Polská
Slezská
Bubenská
Wilsonova
Na poříčí
Hybernská
Italská
Jaroše
Legerova
Sokolská
Veletržní
Celetná
Příkopě
Václavské náměstí
Žitná
Anglická
Ječná
Letenské
Sady
nábřeží
kpt.
Pařížská
VALDŠTEJNSKÁ
ZAHRADA
Národní
Obránců míru
Vltava
Karlův
most
Rašínovo nábře
KRÁLOVSKÁ
ZAHRADA
Letenská
Zborovská
Svorno
Lidická
ZAHRADA NA
VALECH & RAJSKÁ
ZAHRADA
Hradčany
Nerudova
KOLOVRATSKÁ
ZAHRADA
PETŘÍN
Plzeňská
Úvoz
Holečkova
Plzeňská
Plzeňská

ZAHRADA NA VALECH & RAJSKÁ ZAHRADA (WALL GARDENS & PARADISE GARDEN) South side of Prague Castle.
❑ 0900-dusk May-Sep., Sat. & Sun. all year. Tram 22 to Pražský Hrad.
❑ Free.
*Beautiful gardens on the sunny side of the castle (see **Prague Castle**).*

KRÁLOVSKÁ ZAHRADA (ROYAL GARDENS) Between Prague Castle and Belvedere.
❑ 0900-dusk April-Oct. Tram 18, 22. ❑ Kčs 5.
Delightful formal gardens lying between the Belvedere Summer Palace and the castle. The Renaissance Garden contains the 'Singing Fountain' (1564) while the Hercules Fountain (1670) stands in the main garden.

VALDŠTEJNSKÁ ZAHRADA (WALLENSTEIN PALACE GARDENS) Letenská.
❑ 0830-dusk May-Sep. Metro Malostranská; tram 12, 18, 22. ❑ Free.
Magnificent gardens with an Italian loggia – the Sala Terrena – and exquisite statues (now copies) of the Greek Gods by de Vries (1622-26). A popular venue for open-air concerts in summer. See MUSTS.

PETŘÍN (also called Laurenziberg) Malá Strana.
❑ 24 hr. Tram 22, 23 to Strahov district then a short walk, or 12, 22 to U lanové dráhy then the funicular railway (0500-2400; Kčs 4). ❑ Free.
Six former monastery and palace gardens running together to form one huge park. The lookout tower (1891) resembles the Eiffel Tower and offers superb views over the whole city.

VÍTKOV On the far side of Prague's eastern ring road.
❑ 24 hr. Metro Florenc then a short walk or bus 133, 168, 207. ❑ Free.
*An impressive park containing the National Monument (see **A-Z**) and the massive statue of Jan Žižka.*

KOLOVRATSKÁ ZAHRADA (KOLOVRAT PALACE GARDENS) Valdštejnská 10.
❑ 0830-dusk May-Sep. Metro Malostranská; tram 12, 22. ❑ Free.
Unusual and beautiful gardens cascading in terraces. Laid out in 1785.

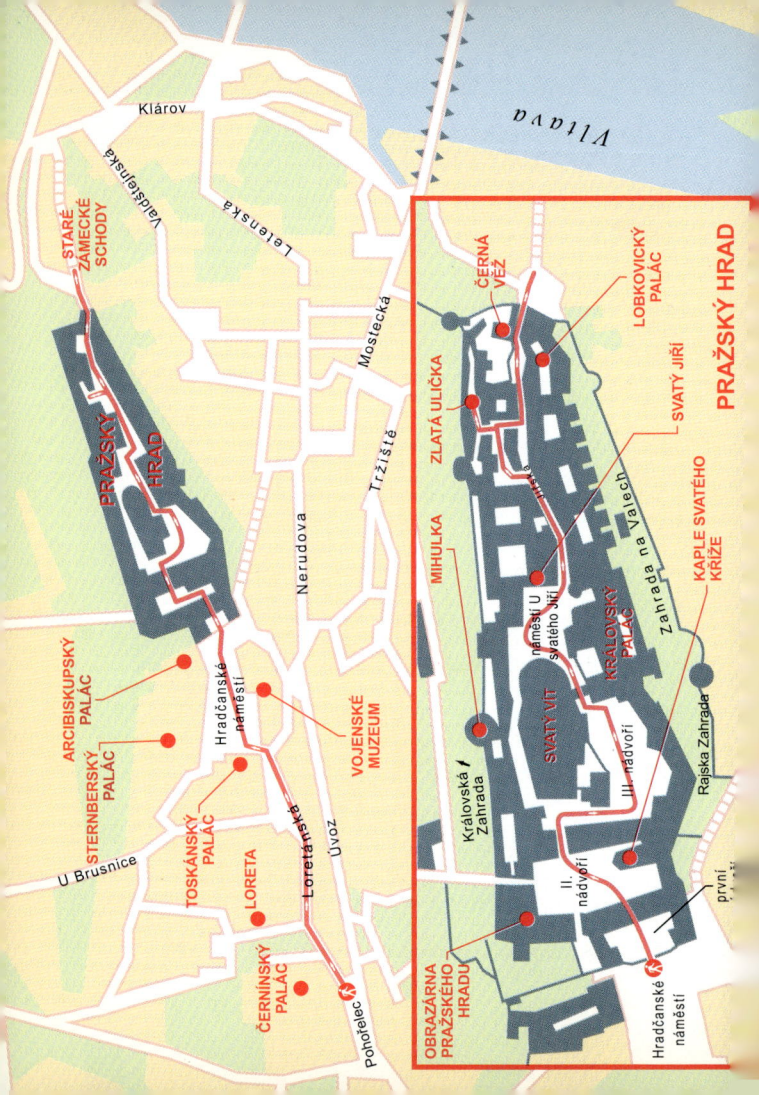

Klárov

Valdštejnská

Letenská

Vltava

STARÉ ZÁMECKÉ SCHODY

PRAŽSKÝ HRAD

Mostecká

Tržiště

Nerudova

ARCIBISKUPSKÝ PALÁC

STERNBERSKÝ PALÁC

Hradčanské náměstí

VOJENSKÉ MUZEUM

TOSKÁNSKÝ PALÁC

U Brusnice

LORETA

Loretánská

Úvoz

ČERNÍNSKÝ PALÁC

Pohořelec

PRAŽSKÝ HRAD

ČERNÁ VĚŽ

LOBKOVICKÝ PALÁC

ZLATÁ ULIČKA

SVATÝ JIŘÍ

MIHULKA

náměstí U svatého Jiří

Zahrada na Valech

KAPLE SVATÉHO KŘÍŽE

Královská Zahrada

SVATÝ VÍT

KRÁLOVSKÝ PALÁC

III. nádvoří

Rajská Zahrada

II. nádvoří

první

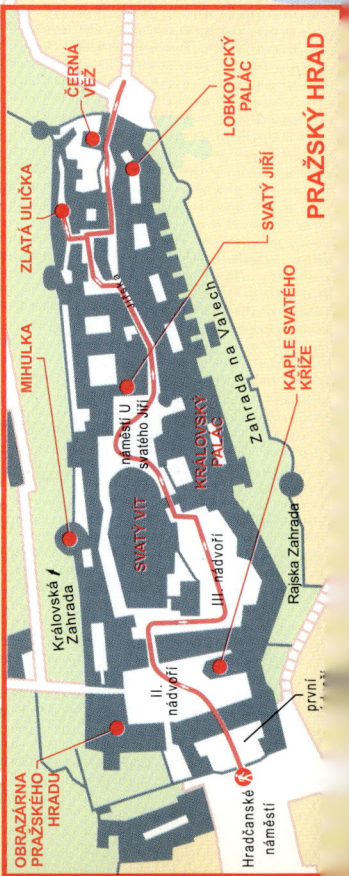

OBRAZÁRNA PRAŽSKÉHO HRADU

Hradčanské náměstí

A full-day exploration of this huge site which dominates the city centre.

Prague Castle and the district known as Hradčany (castle town) warrant a full-day's excursion in their own right simply because there is so much to see. Begin by taking tram 22 from Národní in the centre of town up to the top of the hill and alight at Pohořelec, a pretty square reminiscent of that in a country town. To your right is the Strahovský klášter (Strahov Monastery – see **A-Z**) with its magnificent library. Walk back into the square and to your left you will see the massive Czernin (Černínský) Palace and the Loreto Church (Loreta) in Loretánské náměstí. Carry on down Loretánska until you reach Hradčanské náměstí – Castle Sq. On the left you will pass three palaces; Toskánský, Arcibiskupský and Šternberský, while to the right stands the Schwarzenberg's stately home, now the Army Museum (Vojenské Muzeum). In front of you stands the main entrance to the castle. Passing the smart guards on duty you will enter the First Courtyard (první nádvoří), also called Nobles' Court. Pass through the archway known as the Matthias Gate, built in 1614 by Scamozzi, and you will find yourself in the Second Courtyard. The glass doors under the archway lead to the private apartments of the President of the Republic. You are now facing the Holy Cross Chapel (kaple svatého Kříže – 1753) in which are housed many of the great national treasures originally in St. Vitus' Cathedral, including personal objects of St. Wenceslas (see **Good King Wenceslas**). On the other side of the courtyard is the Castle Picture Gallery, housed in the former stables. In the centre is a splendid baroque fountain by Kohl (1686). Pass under the central archway and enter the Third Courtyard where the immense form of St. Vitus' Cathedral rears up in front of you. Make sure you see St. Wenceslas' Chapel, built by the German architect Peter Parler (see **A-Z**) in 1367. Both he and Matthias of Arras (see **A-Z**), who were the principal designers of this magnificent building, are buried in the Wallenstein chapel near the high altar. To the left of the cathedral stands the Chancellery (1774) by Pacassi with its famous balcony by Platzer (1761). This has been used by all famous visitors to Prague Castle, welcome or not, and has included Hitler and Mrs Thatcher. Facing the Chancellery is the magnificent South Porch of the cathedral, sometimes called the Golden Gate, with its very

Prague Old Town

unusual mosaic crafted by Venetian workmen in 1371. What makes it so unusual is that it is made of glass chips, not stone. Between the end of the Chancellery and the cathedral, in the corner of the courtyard stands the entrance to the former Royal Palace, the Královský Palác. The most impressive part is the huge medieval hall known as the Vladislav Hall. It was built in 1493-1502 by Ried and, with Westminster Hall, is one of the largest in Europe. Its 62 m length was used for indoor jousting tournaments among other things. In the Green Room is the famous window, where in 1618, some prominent citizens were thrown out! See also the Allhallows Chapel, The Old Diet Chamber (Stará sněmovna) and the Knights' Stairway, as well as the undercroft (1140) of the old palace. On leaving the palace enter St. George's Courtyard where you will find, facing you, the ancient church of St. George (svatý Jiří). Tucked behind that is St. George's Convent (Jiřský klášter), now home to the Old Bohemian Collection of the National Gallery. Just visible to the right of St. Vitus' Cathedral, from where you are, is the Vikářská and in it, a small round tower (1480) known as the Mihulka (Powder Tower) where an interesting show of Renaissance technology is on permanent display. There is also an excellent restaurant here. Walk down George's Alley (Jiřská ulička), until it opens out into a small square. You will see a sign which reads 'Zlatá ulička', and past an art gallery on your left, find Golden Lane with its tiny attractive houses. Return to Jiřská ulička and follow the slope down, until on your right, you will see the old Lobkowicz Palace where there is a display on the history of Bohemia. At the end of the alley, straddling the gateway, is the Black Tower (Černá věž), part of the 12thC fortifications. From here you can return to the river level down the Old Castle Steps (Staré zámecké schody) where there are many traders selling excellent and inexpensive etchings of old Prague. There are also magnificent views over the city from the little square just outside the gateway. In fine weather you may wish to visit the various gardens in the complex, but for the average visitor this will already be enough for one day. The only parts of the castle that cannot be visited at the moment are the President's quarters and, sadly, the magnificent Spanish hall and Rudolf's Gallery, often used for official functions. See **ART GALLERIES, CASTLES & PALACES 1 & 2, CHURCHES 1 & 2, MUSEUMS, Prague Castle**.

Bubenské nábřeží

Ostrov Štvanice

Sokolovská

Křižíkova

Táboritská

Ondříčkova

Vinohradská

Korunní

Seifertova

Slezská

Polská

Italská

Bubenská

Wilsonova

Na poříčí

Hybernská

ALEX

PEKING

Legerova

Sokolská

Veletržní

Jaroše

PRAHA-EXPO 1958 TERRACE RESTAURANT

Celetná

Na příkopě

RYBÁRNA

Václavské náměstí

MAYUR

Žitná

Anglická

Ječná

nábřeží kpt.

Letenské Sady

Pařížská

BERJOZKA

Národní

Rašínovo nábř.

Obránců míru

Vltava

Karlův most

Letenská

Zborovská

Lidická

Svorn

Hradčany

Nerudova

TRATTORIA VIOLA

Petřín

Holečkova

Plzeňská

Úvoz

Plaňří

PEKING I. P. Pavlova, tel: 293531.
❏ 1130-1500, 1730-2000, 2030-2300 Mon.-Sat. Metro I.P. Pavlova, 1st flight of steps to the right; tram 4, 6, 11, 16, 22. ❏ Moderate-expensive.
Good-value, authentic Chinese dishes. Popular, so essential to book.

PRAHA-EXPO 1958 TERRACE RESTAURANT Letenské sady, tel: 377339.
❏ French restaurant 1300-1500, 1800-2300; Pilsen restaurant 1130-1600, 1700-2300. Tram 5, 12, 14, 17, 26; best by taxi. ❏ Moderate.
Two superb restaurants – one French, the other offering Czech specialities – and a café. Excellent quality meats are served here.

RYBÁRNA Václavské náměstí 43, tel: 227741.
❏ Baltic Grill 1000-2330 Sun.-Fri.; fish restaurant 1100-2200 Mon.-Sat. Metro Můstek; tram 3, 9, 24 to Václavské náměstí. ❏ Moderate.
Two restaurants in one, specializing in fish (the Grill also serves meat dishes). Try the kapr *(carp),* pstruh *(trout) or the speciality of the day.*

ALEX Revoluční 11, tel: 2314489.
❏ 1130-1600, 1700-2400. Metro Náměstí Republiky; tram 5, 14, 26. ❏ Moderate.
Good-value, hearty German fare. Excellent pork chops, sauerkraut, etc.

TRATTORIA VIOLA Národní 7, tel: 266732.
❏ 1200-2400. Metro Můstek; tram 6, 9, 18, 21, 22. ❏ Moderate.
Popular Italian restaurant. Essential to book a table.

BERJOZKA Rytířská 31, tel: 223822.
❏ 1100-2300. Metro Můstek; tram 6, 9, 18 then walk through from Národní. ❏ Inexpensive.
Good Russian restaurant serving dishes like borsch and blini (pancakes).

MAYUR Štěpánská 61, tel: 2369922.
❏ 1200-1600, 1800-2300 Mon.-Sat. Metro Muzeum; tram 3, 9, 24 to Václavské náměstí. ❏ Inexpensive.
Good-value Indian dishes; a welcome change from Prague dumplings!

Bubenské nábřeží
Ostrov Štvanice
Sokolovská
Křižíkova
Bubenská
Jaroše
Veletržní
Letenské Sady
nábřeží kpt. Jaroše
Obránců míru
Pionýrů
Hradčany
Úvoz
Nerudova
Letenská
Vltava
Pařížská
Celetná
Na příkopě
Na poříčí
Hybernská
Wilsonova
Seifertova
Táboritská
Odřiškovova
Italská
Polská
Vinohradská
Slezská
Korunní
Legerova
Sokolská
Žitná
Anglická
Ječná
Václavské náměstí
Národní
Karlův most
Petřín
Zborovská
Rašínovo nábř
Lidická
Svorn
Plzeňská
Holečkova

OBECNÍ DŮM
U SV. TOMÁŠE
DRUŽBA
U FLEKŮ
U MECENÁŠE
U LABUTÍ
U LORETY

Traditional

U LABUTÍ Hradčanské náměstí 11, tel: 539476.
❏ 0900-2300 Mon.-Sat. Taxi best. ❏ Moderate-expensive.
Offers a wide-ranging menu, with venison and other meats a speciality.
Delightful atmosphere. Booking is recommended.

U FLEKŮ Křemencova 9, tel: 293246.
❏ 0830-2300. Metro Národní třída then walk up Spálená into Myslíkova;
tram 3, 6, 18, 21, 22, 24 to Karlovo náměstí. ❏ Moderate.
Best-known beer hall in Prague. Serves good basic food; has live music.

U LORETY Loretánské náměstí 8, next door to the church opposite
Czernin Palace, tel: 536025.
❏ 1100-1500, 1800-2300 Tue.-Sun. Tram 22, 23. ❏ Moderate.
Plain simple fare and known for its local wine selection (see **Wines***).*

OBECNÍ DŮM Náměstí Republiky 1090, tel: 2311268.
❏ 1130-2300. Metro Náměstí Republiky; tram 5, 14, 26.
❏ Moderate.
Good restaurant within the Municipal House (see **A-Z***). The pork chops*
are excellent, as are the desserts.

DRUŽBA Václavské náměstí 16.
❏ 0900-2300. Metro Můstek; tram 3, 9, 24. ❏ Moderate.
Excellent restaurant serving Bohemian specialities such as Prague ham,
braised beef, sweet dumplings, etc. (see **Food***).*

U MECENÁŠE Malostranské náměstí 10, tel: 533881.
❏ 1700-2400 Sun.-Fri. Metro Malostranská; tram 12, 22.
❏ Moderate.
Medieval-type restaurant with genuine antique furniture and a great atmo-
sphere. Ham is the speciality and the dumplings are excellent.

U SV. TOMÁŠE Letenská 12, tel: 530064.
❏ 0800-2400. Metro Malostranská; tram 12, 22. ❏ Inexpensive.
Delightfully located ancient tavern with its own brewery tap
(Branik 12%).

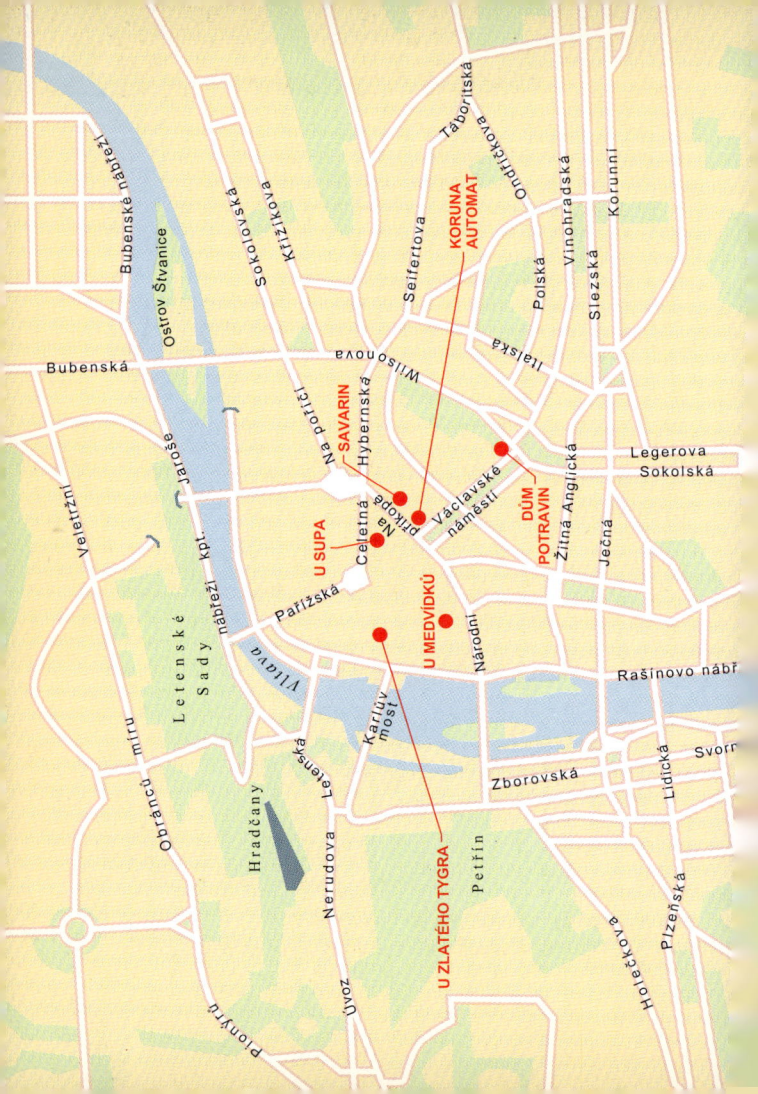

KORUNA AUTOMAT

SAVARIN

DŮM POTRAVIN

U ŠUPA

U MEDVÍDKŮ

U ZLATÉHO TYGRA

Legerova
Sokolská

Bubenské nábřeží

Bubenská

Ostrov Štvanice

Sokolovská

Křižíkova

Na poříčí

Hybernská

Wilsonova

Seifertova

Táboritská

Ondříčkova

Vinohradská

Polská

Slezská

Korunní

Italská

Václavské náměstí

Žitná

Anglická

Ječná

Na příkopě

Celetná

Pařížská

Jaroše

nábřeží kpt.

Veletržní

Letenské
Sady

Obránců
míru

Hradčany

Vltava

Karlův
most

Letenská

Nerudova

Úvoz

Plzeňská

Petřín

Národní

Rašínovo nábř.

Zborovská

Lidická

Svorn

Pizeňská

Holečkova

Plzeňská

Traditional

U MEDVÍDKŮ Na Perštýně 7, tel: 2358904.
❑ 1100-2300 Mon.-Sat. Metro Národní třída; tram 6, 9, 18, 21, 22 to Národní. ❑ Inexpensive.
Typical restaurant and beer house serving southern Bohemian and old Czech specialities; hearty soups, beef stew and dumplings, etc. (see **Food***), and the real Budweiser (see* **Drinks***) strong beer (12%).*

U ZLATÉHO TYGRA Husova 17, tel: 265219.
❑ 1500-2300 Mon.-Sat. Metro Staroměstská; tram 17, 18 to Anenské náměstí, and then follow Anenská into Řetězová. ❑ Inexpensive.
Old-fashioned tavern in the heart of the Old Town (see **A-Z***). Good goulash-type fare with dumplings and sauerkraut. Serves the real Pilsner Urquell in very large glasses.*

SAVARIN Na příkopě 10, tel: 220566.
❑ 1100-1500, 1900-0130 Tue.-Sat. Metro Můstek. ❑ Inexpensive.
Conveniently situated on Prague's main shopping street, this restaurant serves hot meals and snacks, and doubles as a café. Try the rulada *(see* **Food***). It has a summer garden, and holds tea dances.*

DŮM POTRAVIN Corner of Václavské náměstí & Washingtonova.
❑ 0800-2000 Mon.-Fri., 0800-1300 Sat. Metro Muzeum; tram 11. ❑ Inexpensive.
Most unusual delicatessen, coffee house and restaurant in one. Sells delicious open sandwiches and salads, either to take away or eat in-house.

U SUPA Celetná 22, tel: 223042.
❑ 1100-2200. Metro Náměstí Republiky or Můstek; tram 5, 14, 26. ❑ Inexpensive.
Typical Prague restaurant and beer house dating from the 1350s, serving excellent food and fine strong dark beer. Large open hall in summer.

KORUNA AUTOMAT Corner of Václavské náměstí & Na příkopě.
❑ 0830-2300 Mon.-Sat., 0800-1800 Sun. Metro Můstek. ❑ Inexpensive.
Possibly the best known of the automats (see **Eating Out***) which abound near Wenceslas Sq. (see* **A-Z***). Quick service and a high standard of food.*

BOHEMIA-MOSER

BIJOUX DE BOHÈME

DĚTSKÝ DŮM

BOHEMIA

TUZEX

UNIQUE FOLKCRAFT SHOP

HUDEBNINY

Bubenské nábřeží

Ostrov Štvanice

Sokolovská

Křižíkova

Bubenská

Jaroše

Veletržní

Letenské Sady

Obránců míru

nábřeží kpt.

Pařížská

Na poříčí

Hybernská

Wilsonova

Celetná

Na příkopě

Václavské náměstí

Seifertova

Táboritská

Ondříčkova

Polská

Italská

Vinohradská

Korunní

Slezská

Legerova

Sokolská

Žitná

Anglická

Ječná

Vltava

Karlův most

Letenská

Národní

Rašínovo nábř

Hradčany

Nerudova

Úvoz

Pohořelec

Petřín

Zborovská

Lidická

Svorn

Plzeňská

Holečkova

TUZEX Rytířská 13.
❏ 0800-1900. Metro Můstek.
Just one of some 35 Tuzex duty-free stores all over Prague. This one deals in watches, jewellery, etc. Antiques, glass souvenirs, jewellery, paintings and household appliances are all available cheaper than at most airport duty-free shops. There is even a clothing branch at Palackého 13. See **Shopping**.

BOHEMIA-MOSER Na příkopě 12.
❏ 0900-1900 Mon.-Fri., 0900-1300 Sat. Metro Můstek; tram 3, 9, 24.
Superb range of crystal and glassware. The shop has special offers in hard currency, and can arrange shipment of goods.

BOHEMIA Pařížská 1.
❏ 0900-1900 Mon.-Fri., till 1300 Sat. Metro Staroměstská; tram 5, 26.
Excellent glass selection, as well as wall-plates with scenes of Old Prague, porcelain, etc. It is possible to have goods sent to your home.

DĚTSKÝ DŮM Na příkopě 15.
❏ 0830-1900 Mon.-Fri., 0900-1600 Sat. Metro Můstek; tram 3, 9, 24.
Wonderful selection of children's toys at very reasonable prices. Specializes in wooden playthings, etc.

UNIQUE FOLKCRAFT SHOP Betlémské náměstí 2.
❏ 0900-1900 Mon.-Fri., 1000-1800 Sat., 1100-1800 Sun. Metro Národní třída or Staroměstská; tram 17, 18.
Unrivalled selection of table linen, etc. much of it handcrafted. Also sells wooden knick-knacks, prints of Old Prague and decorative candles.

HUDEBNINY Újezd 15.
❏ 0900-1800 Mon.-Fri., 0900-1500 Sat. Tram 6, 9, 12, 22.
Ideal for the music-lover, a wide range of sheet music at very low cost.

BIJOUX DE BOHÈME Staroměstské náměstí 22.
❏ 0800-2000 Mon.-Fri., 0900-1700 Sat., Sun. Metro Staroměstská.
Good selection of semiprecious stones, for which Bohemia is famous.

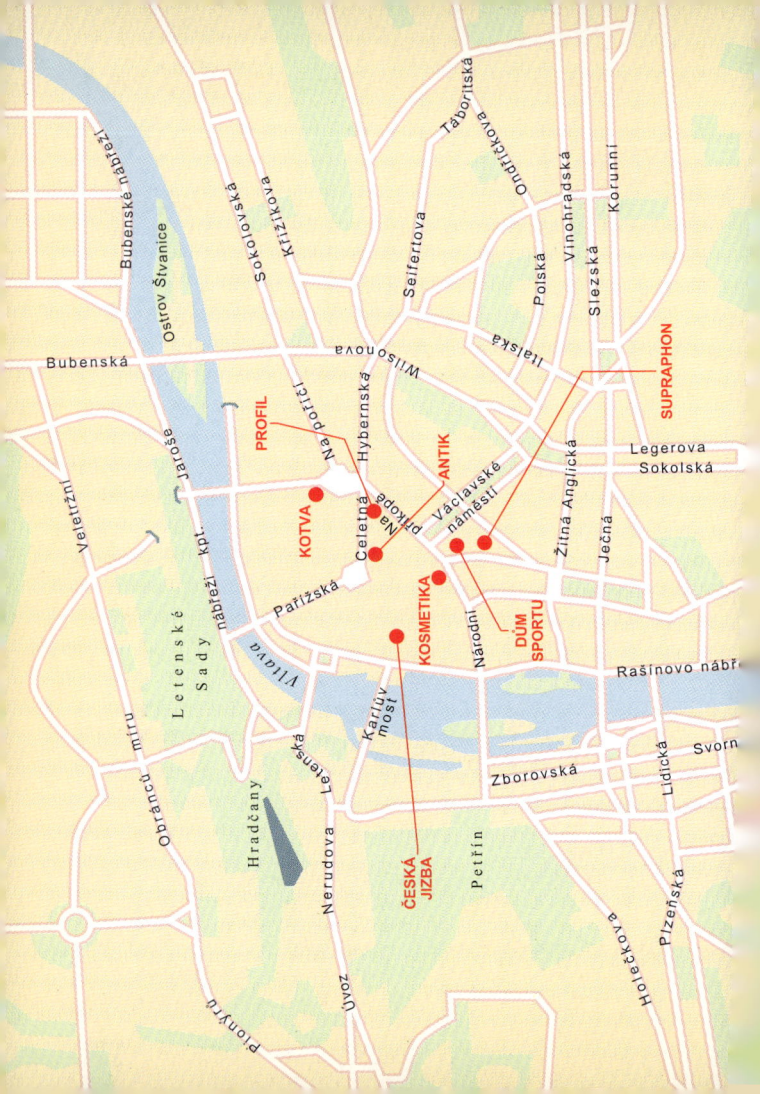

KOTVA Revoluční, on the corner of náměstí Republiky.
❏ 0800-1900 Mon.-Fri., 0800-1800 Sat. Metro Náměstí Republiky; tram 5, 14, 26.
This is the largest department store in Prague. The choice is limited by Western standards, but there are many bargains including gifts and souvenirs.

ČESKÁ JIZBA Karlova 12.
❏ 0900-1800 Mon.-Fri. Metro Staroměstská; tram 17, 18.
Small store near the Old Town Sq. with an excellent selection of gifts: handicrafts, dolls, ornamental plaques, etc.

ANTIK Celetná 31.
❏ 0830-1900 Mon.-Fri., 0830-1300 Sat. Metro Náměstí Republiky or Staroměstská.
Specialists in all kinds of coins, especially those of the Austro-Hungarian Empire and Bohemia.

PROFIL Na příkopě 24 (in the arcade at this number).
❏ 1000-1800 Mon.-Fri. Metro Můstek.
Excellent selection of stamps (bought and sold). It's worth looking around even if you are not purchasing.

DŮM SPORTU Jungmannova 28.
❏ 0830-1900 Mon.-Sat. Metro Národní třída; tram 6, 9, 18, 21, 22.
Splendid range of sports articles at very reasonable prices. See **Sports***.*

SUPRAPHON Palackého 1.
❏ 1000-1800 Mon.-Sat. Metro Národní třída; tram 3, 9, 24.
Best place in Prague to buy CDs or LP records of excellent quality at bargain prices. Classics are the best buys of all.

KOSMETIKA 28 října 5.
❏ 0900-1800 Mon.-Fri., till 1200 Sat. Metro Můstek; tram 9, 18, 21, 22.
Virtually unknown brands for Western visitors, but toiletries of good quality and price available.

Vltava

Na Františku

STARONOVÁ
SYNAGÓGA

ŽIDOVSKÁ
RADNICE

Pařížská

Kozí

Haštalská

Kozí

Revoluční

Rybná

Maiselova

Široká

KOSTEL
SVATÉHO
MIKULÁŠE

KOSTEL PANNY
MARIE PŘED TÝNEM

KINSKÝ
PALÁC

náměstí
Republiky

Staroměstské
náměstí

Celetná

MAISELOVÁ
SYNAGÓGA

Železná

Karlova

Melantrichova

STAVOVSKÉ
DIVADLO

PRAŠNÁ
BRÁNA

KAROLINUM

STAROMĚSTSKÁ
RADNICE

Havelská

Rytířská

Na můstku

Na Příkopě

M

28. října

Václavské
náměstí

1 hr, excluding visits to museums, churches, etc.
Begin the walk from Metro Můstek at the bottom end of Václavské náměstí (see **Wenceslas Square**). Walk down the little pedestrianized alleyway called Na můstku into Rytířská (Knights St). To your right, at the end of the street, you will see the Estates Theatre (Stavovské divadlo) where Mozart's *Don Giovanni* was first performed in 1787 (see **Mozart**). To the left of the theatre is the Karolinum (Carolinum – see **A-Z**), founded in 1348. Continue down Melantrichova and pause at the Havelská crossing to see the street market and admire the old houses, some with arcades. Go straight on and you come to Staroměstské náměstí (Old Town Sq.) where you will be facing Staroměstská radnice (Old Town Hall – see **A-Z**) and the Astronomical Clock (see **CHILDREN**, **A-Z**). Diagonally across to your right are the Týn Church (kostel Panny Marie před Týnem – see **CHURCHES 1**) and the Kinský Palace (see **ART GALLERIES**, **CASTLES & PALACES 2**). In the centre of the square is the monument to Jan Hus (see **A-Z**) and the other Protestant martyrs. The square was not only a major place of execution but also an international marketplace. Behind the Týn Church is the Toll yard (Týn or Ungelt) where the merchants paid their dues. In the other corner of the square you will see the elegant white outline of St. Nicholas' Church (kostel svatého Mikuláše – see **CHURCHES 2**), while the row of 18th and 19thC houses in front of you is typical of Prague as it used to be. Now cross the square and have a look at the massive chandelier in St. Nicholas' Church. On the corner of Maiselova is the house where Kafka (see **A-Z**) was born. Continue down Maiselova where, on your right,

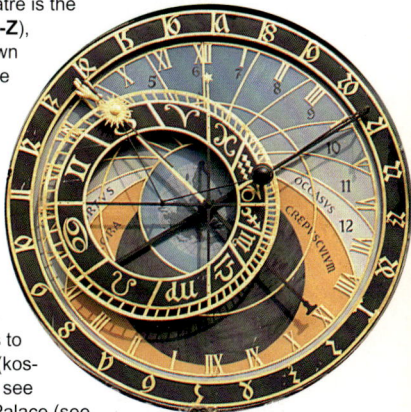

you will pass the Maisel Synagogue. Cross Široká and you will find, on the right, the Jewish Town Hall (Židovská radnice) and the Old-New Synagogue (Staronová synagóga – see **OLD JEWISH TOWN**). Go down the alleyway between the two buildings and you are in Pařížská, one of the main streets in Prague for airline offices and other up-market enterprises. To your left you can make out the modern shape of the Intercontinental Hotel. Turn right and return towards the Old Town Sq. Cross diagonally to the furthest corner left, which is the beginning of Celetná (Baker St) and note the extremely attractive houses facing you. The last house on the right, which is painted grey and white, was once the music school run by the great composer Smetana (see **A-Z**). Celetná forms part of the old 'Royal Way', from the residence near the Powder Tower (see **A-Z**) up to St. Vitus' Cathedral (see **CHURCHES 1, A-Z**) for coronations. The Storch House, at No. 552, has fine wall paintings. Continue up the street where on both sides there are superb old houses and private mansions of every description, such as the baroque palace of the Cavrianis at No. 597. Have a look through the gateway at the courtyard. There are many good wine bars and taverns here, but try the U Supa at No. 22 with its special stout (see **RESTAURANTS 3**). Carry on until you reach the Powder Tower (Prašná brána) at the end of the street. Walk through it, and to your left is náměstí Republiky (Republic Sq.), while to the right is the main shopping street Na příkopě (see **A-Z**) which will lead you back to the start of the walk at Metro Můstek.
See **Old Town**.

Wilsonova

Meziibranská

Legerova

Sokolská

Václavské

náměstí

KOSTEL PANNY MARIE SNĚŽNÉ

Vodičkova

NOVOMĚSTSKÁ RADNICE

Žitná

Anglická

Kateřinská

Ječná

KOSTEL SVATÉHO IGNÁCE

BOTANICKÁ ZAHRADA

Jungmannovo náměstí

Jungmannova

Karlovo náměstí

U nemocnice

KOSTEL SVATÉHO CYRILA A METODĚJE

Myslíkova

Resslova

Vyšehradská

KLÁŠTER NA SLOVANECH

LATERNA MAGICA

Národní

NÁRODNÍ DIVADLO

Jiráskovo náměstí

Jiráskův most

Na Moráni

Masarykovo nábřeží

Slovanský Ostrov

Vltava

Palackého most

Střelecký Ostrov

Dětský Ostrov

1.5 hr, excluding visits to museums, churches, etc.

Start the walk from Metro Muzeum. Come out of the museum exit of the Metro and walk to the front of the building where you will find a ramp. From the top you have an excellent view of the whole 750 m length of Václavské náměstí (Wenceslas Sq. – see **A-Z**) and of the St. Wenceslas monument (see **Good King Wenceslas**). Now the centre of modern Prague, it was in fact first laid out by the ubiquitous Charles IV over 600 years ago. At the far end stands Na příkopě (see **A-Z**), the city's main shopping street. Most of the present buildings in the square date from just before World War I and as you walk down you will find some classic examples of the *Jugendstil* (Art Nouveau) period. Cross the avenue and walk down the left-hand side pausing to look at the Hotels Europa and Ambassador on the right. They are superb examples of the *Jugendstil* style which in other capitals has almost disappeared.

Just as you reach the pedestrianized section by the Můstek Metro station at the very end of the square, turn left into the passage which leads you to Jungmannovo náměstí. Just before the statue to the great Czech linguist, turn left and enter the small courtyard by the arch which brings you to the front of kostel Panny Marie Sněžné (St. Mary of the Snows – see **CHURCHES 2**). Note the very Eastern mosaic of the Madonna and Child over the doorway. On the opposite corner of the square, facing the statue, is the old Adria Palace Hotel complex. This is the beginning of Národní třída (National Ave) in which the headquarters of many offices are located as well as one of Prague's major department stores, Máj, and at No.4 the Laterna Magica theatre (see **CHILDREN**). If you feel hungry or need a beer either call in at U Pinkasů, a typical tavern, or continue to the end of the street where close by the National Theatre (Národní divadlo) you will find the most unusual wine bar in a former Ursuline convent aptly named Klášterní vinárna (Convent Wine Bar)!

Vltava

Turn left and follow Masarykovo nábřeží along the embankment of the Vltava (see **A-Z**), from where you will notice several islands in the river. The nearest is called Slovanský Ostrov, because the first Pan-Slavic conferences were held there in 1848. On the same island Berlioz, Wagner and Liszt all gave concerts. At the next intersection, Jiráskovo náměstí, turn left into Resslova, where you will see two large churches practically facing each other. The one to your left at the junction of Na Zderaze is the former Charles Borromeo church now dedicated to Saints Cyril and Methodius (kostel svatého Cyrila a Metoděje). Note the bullet marks around the crypt windows where flowers are usually placed, even in winter. It was here that the attackers of Heydrich made their last stand against the SS in May 1942 (see **Lidice**). Resslova now enters Karlovo náměstí (Charles Sq.) approximately at the centre of the square. From where you stand you cannot fail to miss, on the opposite side, the massive outline of St. Ignatius Church (kostel svatého Ignáce) with its gold-leaf decoration. It was built for the Jesuits in 1699. Continue down the right-hand side of the square and follow the tram

Wenceslas Square

tracks until you reach the lower end where it joins U nemocnice. At No.
40 stands the Faust House (Faustův dům), formerly a palace and now a
pharmacy.

Just a little further along on your right, in the street called Vyšehradská,
stands the former Benedictine monastery, klášter Na Slovanech, built in
the 14thC. It is particularly worth seeing for its strange towers, built to
replace the originals which were destroyed by bombs during an air raid
at the very end of World War II. It houses some interesting early frescoes (1360) in the cloisters. You could also spend a pleasant hour or so
visiting the Botanical Gardens (Botanická zahrada) which are open
every day from 0900-dusk (summer only), admission free. From here
return along the right-hand side of Karlovo náměstí, passing the New
Town Hall (Novoměstská radnice), built 1374-1498. It was the scene of
many confrontations between the reformers of Jan Hus (see **A-Z**) and
the city council in the 1420s. Walk along Vodičkova at the side of the
New Town Hall, then along Jungmannova to return to Jungmannovo
náměstí and the bottom of Václavské náměstí. See **New Town**.

Map labels:

Křižovnické náměstí

Křižovnická

Smetanovo nábřeží

KOSTEL PANNY MARIE POD ŘETĚZEM

KARLŮV MOST

Mánesův most

Vltava

Střelecký Ostrov

KAMPA

VALDŠTEJNSKÝ PALÁC

Valdštejnská

Letenská

Malostranské náměstí

Mostecká

Maltézské náměstí

Vítězná

Pražský Hrad

MALOSTRANSKÁ KAVÁRNA

Karmelitská

Újezd

Nerudova

Tržiště

VRTBOVSKÁ ZAHRADA

KOSTEL PANNY MARIE VÍTĚZNÉ

Petřínské Sady

FUNICULAR RAILWAY

CHRÁM SVATÉHO MIKULÁŠE

Vlašská

Hradčanské náměstí

P e t ř í n

Loretánská

Úvoz

Pohořelec

Strahovská

Charles Bridge & the Lesser Town

1.5 hr, excluding visits to museums, churches, etc.
Begin the walk at Křížovnické náměstí, at the foot of Charles Bridge
(see **CHILDREN**, **A-Z**). Pass under the Old Town Tower of the bridge and
admire the view up to Prague Castle (see **PRAGUE CASTLE**, **A-Z**) on the
hill above you. Charles Bridge (Karlův most) is one of the most famous
in the world and certainly one of the oldest in Europe still in regular use.
It was built under Charles IV's orders in 1357 by the German architect
Peter Parler (see **A-Z**) and is lined by 30 statues, mostly saints associated with Prague. Now closed to vehicular traffic, try to imagine how it
must have looked in earlier centuries – busy with horses, trades folk and
carriages of every description. Passing under the Lesser Town Tower at
the far side of the bridge you will find yourself in the street called
Mostecká (Bridgefoot), which has numerous shops, cafés and restaurants. At Lázenská turn left, and you will shortly find yourself in
Maltézské náměstí (Malta Sq.). Beethoven stayed at No. 11, the former
Wolkenstein Palace, in 1796 when it had become the guesthouse called
At the Golden Unicorn.
The church opposite is kostel Panny Marie pod řetězem (St. Mary under
the Chain), built in the 12thC for the Knights of Malta whose Grand Prior
has his palace next door. The present building dates from 1738 and
until recently housed the Musical Instrument Museum. Carry on past the
Prior's House and you will see the Palais Buquoy-Longueval (1628),
now the French Embassy. At the end of the little square a small bridge
takes you onto the delightful Kampa Island (see **A-Z**) where there are
many attractive houses and gardens, as well as a water mill,
Velkopřevorský mlýn (1598), which once ground the grain for the
Maltese knights. Walk back to Maltézské náměstí and take Harantova
which will bring you into Karmelitská practically facing the old Carmelite
church of kostel Panny Marie Vítězné (Our Lady of the Victories – see
A-Z). In this church (to the right of the central nave) you can see the
famous tiny statue of the Infant Jesus of Prague, beloved by the faithful
who come here from all over the world to see it. In this street at No.
18/379, on the right just before Prokopská, was the famous inn – At the
Black Lion – where among others, Nelson and Lady Hamilton stayed on
a visit to Prague in the autumn of 1800. Today it is an archive and cannot be visited.

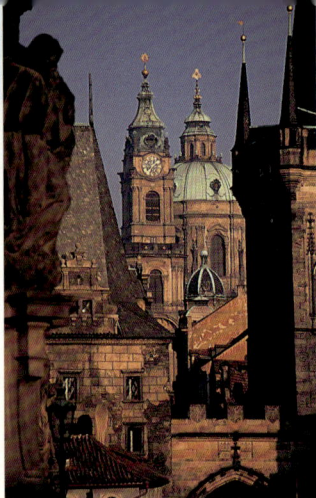

After visiting Our Lady of the Victories, you can either take the funicular railway (see **CHILDREN**) to the top of Petřín park (see **PARKS & GARDENS**) or turn to the left off Karmelitská and visit the Vrtba Palace Gardens (Vrtbovská zahrada). Otherwise, continue along Karmelitská passing, on your left, a street called Tržiště where the American Embassy is located at No. 15 (Shirley Temple Black is the present ambassador). Take the second turning on the left, at the side of St. Nicholas' Church, and you will enter a glorious square with one of the Liechtenstein Palaces in front of you and the church to your right. Chrám svatého Mikuláše (St. Nicholas' Church – see **CHURCHES 1**, **A-Z**) is one of the biggest churches in Prague. Cross the square and walk up Nerudova towards the castle. This is probably one of the most typical streets in Prague and contains many splendid houses and palaces – now embassies – such as the Thun-Hohenstein stately home. You will see it halfway up the street on the right and practically opposite the Morzin Palace which is now the Romanian Embassy. At No. 47 in this street stands At the Two Suns which was once one of the most famous inns in Prague. This is where Neruda wrote *Tales of the Lesser Town,* hence the plaque and the name of the street. Return through St. Nicholas Sq. following Nerudova until it enters the very historic and attractive Lesser Town Sq. (Malostranské náměstí) where you can take refreshment at the former Kleinseitner Café, now the Malostranská Kavárna (see **CAFÉS**). If you wish to make this into a half-day outing, this would be an ideal opportunity to explore the dozens of small streets and alleyways that make up the Lesser Town (see **A-Z**). Now either return to Charles Bridge by Mostecká, to the right of the square, or follow the tram tracks into Letenská and visit the Wallenstein Palace (Valdštejnský Palác – see **CASTLES & PALACES 2**). Cross the bridge to return to the start of the walk.

Charles Bridge

Accidents & Breakdowns: In the case of an accident without any casualties, fill out the international self-copying form provided by your insurance company, keeping one copy for yourself. The green card insurance document will save you much time and energy, especially with language problems. If there are casualties call the police on 158 and send for an ambulance (although usually Autoturist will do this automatically for you). There are SOS phones along all major roads in Czechoslovakia and Autoturist offers a network of breakdown and repair services to stranded motorists. Their central dispatch office in Prague will also help you in either English or German, tel: 224906. Breakdown crews are known as the 'Yellow Angels' because they arrive in bright yellow Škodas. There are 24-hr breakdown services in Prague at Malešice or Limuzská 12, tel: 773455; emergency number 154. They can provide a detailed list of garages in the city that deal exclusively with Western makes of car. See **Driving**, **Emergency Numbers**.

Accommodation: Prague has a large number of hotels for a city of its size but due to the very great increase in visitors who now wish to see the city since the Iron Curtain was lifted, they are often fully booked from Mar.–mid Nov. This is particularly true of the more popular three-star establishments. Rooms tend to be rather small, but standards of cleanliness are excellent. Čedok Tours in London can help with booking in advance (17-18 Old Bond St, London, W1X 4RB, tel: 071-6296058) or if you arrive in Prague and need accommodation, try Pragotur's office at U Obecního Domu, náměstí Republiky (Republic Sq.), opposite the Hotel Paříž. One of the services they offer is to arrange accommodation in the home of a Czech family (expect to pay around Kčs 900-1200 for a room) which will include a voucher for breakfast at a nearby restaurant. This accommodation can only be arranged after 1700 on the day of arrival and you must go in person. You could also try AVE at Wilsonova 80, CS-12106-Prague 2, tel: 2362560/2363075 (0600-2330 daily), or at their office in Prague main-line station (see **Railways**), open till 2200 every day. This is a private company and their service is a little more flexible than Pragotur.

If you arrive by car, you will find endless signs, in German, along all routes indicating 'Zimmer Frei' ('Room Free') in a private home (with a breakfast included). You can inspect the room and will be surprised by the high standard offered. Lastly, if you are really desperate, go to the Prague Information Service desk, Na příkopě 20.

Prague also has a very well provided system of Botels – floating hotels on the Vltava river (see **A-Z**). Ask your travel agent or Čedok for details. See **Camping & Caravanning**, **Students**, **Tourist Information**.

Airport: Prague's international airport is at Ruzyně, 19 km northwest of the city centre (journey time about 25 min). Domestic flights are also handled here. There are two airport bus services. One is run by Czech Airlines (ČSA) in conjunction with Cedok (see **Tourist Information**) and calls at all the main hotels – your concierge will give you details. The fare at present is Kčs 10, but sometimes this is included in package deals and airline ticket prices. The other, independent, service is run by the airport authority and ČSA as a special bus service. It runs to and from the airport terminal at Revoluční 25 (at the river end of the avenue) at half-hourly intervals until 1900, costing Kčs 10. Taxis (see **A-Z**) also run to and from the airport. Most of the main airline offices are in Pařížská avenue and you can contact ČSA for international flight information on 2312595 or 2352785. There is a Central Information Service for all other airlines at the airport, tel: 367814 or 367760. If you have any difficulty with language or you need direct consultation with the airline, it is best to go through your hotel concierge. The British Airways office in town is at Štěpánská 63, just off the centre of Wenceslas Sq., tel: 2360353. To contact them at the airport, tel: 367731. Lufthansa (Prague) tel: 2317440, (airport) tel: 367827. Air France (Prague) tel: 260155, (airport) tel: 367819. See **Car Hire**.

Astronomical Clock: Prague's astronomical clock, on the south side of the Old Town Hall (see **A-Z**) tower, is one of the oldest public timepieces in Europe (1410). It shows not only the time, but also moon phases, the path of the sun and the signs of the zodiac. Every hour on the hour, the skeleton representing death checks the hourglass before Christ and the 12 Apostles come out of the left-hand, hatch-like door. They then proceed round into the right-hand entrance, with the last of them, Judas, turning his back. When this has taken place, the top hatch opens and a cockerel appears, flutters and crows. Lastly, Death turns the hourglass over, and sounds a death knell. See **CHILDREN**, **WALK 1**.

Baby-sitters: There is no central baby-sitting service in Prague. Ask at your hotel for information. See **CHILDREN**.

Banks: See **Currency**, **Money**, **Opening Times**.

Best Buys: The best buys in Prague are the products for which Bohemia is world-famous, such as glassware, handicrafts and toys. The art of glass-making was brought to Bohemia by German immigrants as early as the 12thC and this area had all the natural raw materials required. It was under Rudolf II (see **A–Z**) that a native-born Prague man, Caspar Lehmann (1570-1622), adapted an ancient system for engraving precious stones, to engraving glass. He also pioneered the technique of enamel colouring in the glass that was to become the hall-mark of Bohemian crystal. Porcelain is very good value, as are table linen in traditional designs, ornamental candles, prints and certain food items like Prague ham in tins (see **Food**). Prague has a long and che-quered history and so has plenty of antiques. A lot of the restrictions concerning the sale of antiques have recently been lifted along with the Iron Curtain, although they still usually come under the umbrella of the duty-free group Tuzex (see **SHOPPING 1**) with the shops under several different names such as Dílo. However, private antique shops are starting to appear. For visitors using hard currency, Prague is a very good place to buy records and tapes, especially of classical music. Lastly, as a souvenir for those at home and also for your own coffee table, you will not find cheaper, more expertly printed picture books anywhere to com-pare with those in Prague, showing superb shots of the whole city, the castle, and the Bohemian countryside. See **SHOPPING 1 & 2**, **Shopping**.

Bethlehem Chapel (Betlémská kaple): Betlémské náměstí, Old Town. Built in 1391, this chapel is of great historical significance to the Czechs, as it was here that the reformer Jan Hus (see **A-Z**) first preached his ideas which struck a chord for national identity. Mostly demolished in 1786, the chapel was faithfully rebuilt in the 1950s.

Boat Trips: Between May and Sep., you can take boat trips along the Vltava river (see **A-Z**). After Sep., it tends to be on the chilly side (see **Climate**) for this type of excursion. The embarkation spot is located between the two bridges, Jiráskův most and Palackého most. It can be reached by trams 3, 7, 17, 21 which run along the river embankment connecting the National Theatre with the bottom of Vyšehrad hill (see **A-Z**). Prices are very reasonable, around Kčs 25 for a 1-hr tour during which you will see many of the sights from a different angle. Boats leave approximately every 30 min from 0930. Rowing boats can also be hired on Slovanský Ostrov island, a little further along the river, near the National Theatre. For more information on river trips in the city as well as on the lakes beyond (see **EXCURSION 1**) contact the main Čedok office (see **Tourist Information**). A full day out by boat to Slapy and Štěchovice (see **EXCURION 1**) costs around Kčs 300, although the price may vary if a lunch is included. Tel: 293803 to book, and if you have language difficulties ask at your hotel for help.

Bohemia: This is the name given to the westernmost provinces of Czechoslovakia by all but the Czechs themselves. Prague is the chief town in this area as well as being capital of the country formed after World War I by amalgamating Bohemia with Moravia and Slovakia. Bohemia takes its name from the Boii, a Celtic tribe who inhabited the region during the period of the Roman Empire. The Slav Czechs arrived later, intermingling and often intermarrying, until the Boii disappeared in all but name.

Budget:

Three-course meal	Kčs 120-300
Glass of beer	Kčs 10-20
Glass of wine	Kčs 25-35
Coffee	Kčs 10-15
Taxi (3 km)	Kčs 35 (approx.)
Transport	Kčs 4
Theatre ticket	Kčs 55

Buses: See **Transport**.

Cameras & Photography: All the main international brands of film are available in Prague, although they are more expensive than in the West. There are plenty of good developing services all over the city and print costs are much cheaper than at home. There is also a very good film and camera shop in the middle of Celetná practically opposite the wine bar U Zlatého Jelena (The Golden Deer). Note that Czech chemists (see **A-Z**) do not sell film. Look for shops displaying the word 'Foto' or the familiar Kodak or Agfa signs.

Camping & Caravanning: Czechoslovakia is an ideal country for camping and good uncluttered roads make for relaxed touring with a caravan. There are several camp sites within the city and in the sur-rounding areas: Caravan, Prague 9-Kbely, Mladoboleslavská 72, tel: 892532, is a good site located in the suburbs, with all facilities; Caravan Camp TJ Vysoké Skoly, Prague 5, Plzeňská, tel: 524714, is also a good site on the main road from Plzeň (see **A-Z**) and the border. Čedok

(see **Tourist Information**) can provide a complete list of camp sites in
and around the city. Members of the Caravan Club can order a list of
the sites and facilities in Czechoslovakia from The Caravan Club, East
Grinstead House, London Rd, East Grinstead, Sussex RH19 1UA,
priced £5.95 inc. p & p. Before you travel it would be best to contact
Čedok in London for their advice (and information on all facilities), especially as the laws relating to the temporary importation of caravans is
under review at the moment.

Car Hire: Most of the international car-hire firms are starting to open up
in Czechoslovakia, some with offices via agents in the city centre, while
others have a desk at the airport (see **A-Z**). However, you will get a
much better deal if you book your car at home and pay in advance for a
Sterling Super Save bargain or similar deal. Budget Rent-a-Car offer
extremely good rates for a pre-paid Holiday Drive deal, booked in
advance in the UK, which includes unlimited mileage, insurance and
tax. Otherwise, the price in Prague is around £40 per day for one-two
days' unlimited mileage, reducing to about £29 per day, for a week.
Both British Airways and Czech Airlines run Fly-Drive packages, details
of which you can get from your travel agency or from Čedok in London
(see **Tourist Information**). Budget has a counter at Prague Airport,
tel: 3343253, as well as another in the Czech Airlines office at
Revoluční 1, tel: 2146. At present Avis, Hertz and others are represent-
ed by Pragocar, Štěpánská 42, tel: 2352809 or 2352825. They can also
offer a selection of Czech models at less expensive rates than the
Western equivalents. Contrary to popular belief, the Škoda is an excellent and reliable model and, as it is a national make, service is available
everywhere. You will also find it negotiates the cobbles better than most
cars. You can also ask at your hotel, or the Na příkopě branch of Čedok
for any local bargains.
EC visitors need only their local licence, while visitors from other countries will need an International Driving Licence. All licence holders must
have held their driving qualifications for over a year. By law, you must
keep your licence, car papers, rental agreement and passport with you
at all times. Credit cards are a good way of leaving a deposit. See
Driving, **Insurance**.

Carolinum (Karolinum): What appears from the outside to be a 19thC building is in fact the original faculty of Prague University founded by Charles IV (see **A-Z**) in 1348, and therefore the oldest university in central Europe. The most unusual oriel chapel (1370) is particularly fine. It was extensively renovated in 1968. See **WALK 1**.

Charles IV (1316-78): King of Bohemia and Holy Roman Emperor (1346-78), during whose reign Prague enjoyed a golden age. Charles, who was with his father when he died at Crecy (see **John of Luxemburg**), was educated in France, and as king brought to Prague the best talent in Europe to build his capital. He was responsible for the construction of many of the Prague landmarks still standing today, the most famous perhaps being Charles Bridge (see **A-Z**).

Charles Bridge (Karlův most): One of the major landmarks in the city, the 510 m-long, 10 m-wide bridge spans the Vltava (see **A-Z**) on 16 arches and has done since 1357 when it was begun by the German architect Peter Parler (see **A-Z**). Its 30 statue groups are a wonder in

Charles Bridge, daybreak

themselves, as are the twin towers at each end. From the bridge (sometimes referred to by its German name – Karlsbrücke) there are superb views up to Prague Castle (see **A-Z**). It is located between Mostecká on the Lesser Town (see **A-Z**) side of the river and the end of Karlova in the Old Town (see **A-Z**). See CHILDREN, MUSTS, WALK 3.

Chemists: Czech chemists (*lékárna*) only sell medical preparations while toiletry items are sold in separate shops like drugstores. Chemist shops in the historic centre are not easy to find as modern signs (green cross symbols) are forbidden. Chemists are usually open 0830-1900 Mon.-Fri. and services are good. All medicines are available, if in somewhat strange packaging for Western visitors. Most middle-aged chemists will have at least a grasp of German and younger ones some English too. The pharmacy at Na příkopě 7, tel: 220081, is open practically 24 hr. There are others across the city which stay open late and a list of these is displayed on the doors of chemist shops. Your hotel should be able to help with finding the nearest chemist and any language difficulties. See **Emergency Numbers**, **Health**.

Children: See CHILDREN.

Clementinum (Klementinum): At one time headquarters for the Jesuits in Prague, the Clementinum is the second-largest building in the city (Prague Castle is the largest) and is located on the Old Town (see **A-Z**) side of the river in Mariánské náměstí. It was built 1653-1722 on the site of a former Dominican priory. It encloses five courtyards, four churches, a library and living quarters. The St. Saviour Church stands on one corner facing the Charles Bridge (see **A-Z**), but the rest of the massive plot is now part of the National Library and the University Press. Metro Staroměstská; tram 17, 18.

Climate: Prague sits literally at the heart of Europe and has a classic continental climate of long, hot summers (average temp. 18-27°C) and very cold winters (average temp. minus 2-6°C, as low as minus 13°C at night) with a lot of snow and frost. Spring and autumn tend to be bright but changeable. Autumn in the forests surrounding Prague is an unforgettable sight. Even in midwinter, the city has a special charm with snow and frost on ancient buildings, and all the main sights are still open except, of course, the gardens (see **PARKS & GARDENS**).

Complaints: If you have a complaint about hotel or restaurant service, etc., it is best to take it up with the manager of the premises.

Conversion Chart:

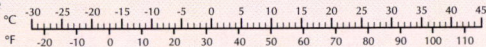

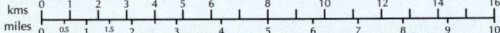

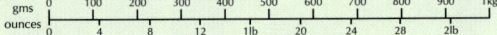

Crime & Theft: By the standards of most Western cities, Prague is certainly not a violent place. Unfortunately, however, certain young groups have seen the Western trappings which they consider smart, and there has been a large increase in bag snatching and stealing of personal stereos and cameras. Be especially careful at all the main tourist spots if you put down your bag while taking photographs. If you do have a problem, there are emergency telephones in many streets and underground stations. Tel: 158 and explain your difficulty. If your passport is lost or stolen contact your embassy. See **Embassies**, **Emergency Numbers**, **Insurance**, **Police**.

Currency: The national currency of Czechoslovakia is the Czechoslovak crown (koruna). The koruna (Kčs) is divided into 100 heller (*halér*). Notes are Kčs 10, 20, 50, 100, 500 and 1000. Coins are Kčs 1, 2, 5 and 10; and 5, 10, 20 and 50 *halér*. See **Money**.

Customs: The Czechs may seem initially to be rather quiet and a little earnest. However, this is only a veneer and you will find that they are very keen to make contact with Western visitors. This is especially true of the younger generation who want to practise their English. Please remember to shake hands at all meetings among friends, but even more so on business. It is considered a major lack of manners not to do so. In bars, restaurants and theatres make sure you hang up your coat rather than drape it over a chair as this is also considered to be in bad taste and comments will be made about 'scruffy' people.

Customs Allowances:

Duty Free Into:	Cigarettes	or	Cigars	or	Tobacco	Spirits	Wine
CZ	250		60		300 g	1*l*	2 *l*
UK	200		50		250 g	1*l*	2 *l*

Czernin Palace (Černínský palác): Standing opposite the Loreto Church (see **Our Lady of Loreto**) in Loretánské náměstí, the palace was one of the largest private residences in Prague. Built 1669-87 for Count Czernin, Austrian envoy to the Republic of Venice, he loved all things Italian and imported architects and workmen to complete it. The palace is now the Foreign Ministry and not open to the public. Tram 22, 23 to Pohořelec.

Dientzenhofer, Christoph (1655-1722) & Kilian (1689-1751): A father and son team of architects who produced some of Prague's most magnificent baroque palaces and churches in the first half of the 18thC. Christoph, and son Kilian, left their legacy in stone all over the city. See **CASTLES & PALACES 2, CHURCHES 1 & 2**.

Disabled People: Facilities for disabled visitors in Czechoslovakia are not entirely of the best, and the hilly layout and many cobbled pavements of Prague do not help. Using trams and buses would also be difficult because of the high step-up. Heavy snow in winter would also bring problems for getting around. See **Health**, **Insurance**.

Doctors: See **Health**.

Drinks: Without doubt the most famous drink in Czechoslovakia is its beer and Czechs are the world's biggest beer drinkers per head of population. Beer bottles around the world carry the famous name of Pilsen (see **EXCURSION 3**, **Plzeň**) far and wide. Of the lager-type beers (much stronger than the British brews and totally different in taste), the names to look for are Pilsner Urquell (Pilsen Original Source) in green bottles and Budweiser in brown (the latter is completely different from the American imitation). Both these brews have kept their old German names and are marketed as such internationally, although you may come across them under their Czech names of Plzeň Prazdroj and Budvar. As well as these internationally-famous brews, there are dozens of others that never leave the country. Prague is famous for its stouts and many of the old-fashioned taverns still serve their own brew (see **RESTAURANTS 3**). It is very powerful stuff and is a cross between Guinness and strong bitter, not unlike the German Alt Bier. Beer is *pivo* in Czech; *světlé* for the light lager-type, and *černé* for the dark variety. The Czechs are also very fond of fruit schnapps of which the most famous is *slivovice*, a clear smooth spirit distilled from plums. Or try some *Becherovka*, a digestive drink which was invented by Dr Becher for his patients at Karlsbad (see **Karlovy Vary**), which also works wonders after a large plate of dumplings (see **Food**)! This strong liqueur is made from honey, herbs and alcohol. Czech wines, almost unheard of outside the country, are very good (see **Wines**). The Czechs also drink a lot of sparkling mineral water (*láhev minerálky – Mineral Wasser* in German), although the tap water in Prague is safe. The coffee is delicious and is served in dozens of different ways. Old habits die hard, so the Viennese coffee (*vídeňská káva*) comes with a thick layer of whipped cream on the top. If you want black coffee ask for *káva*, if you need milk, ask for *mléko*. Tea (*čaj*, pronounced 'cha') tends to be the strong Russian variety, and is quite pleasant once you get used to it. All beverages are available in the cafés and restaurants of Prague at any time as there are no licensing laws.

Driving: The standard international rules apply. Driving is on the right and on suburban roads you must give way to traffic from the right. At roundabouts, the general rule is that traffic on the circus takes priority. Remember to keep your passport, driving licence and car papers with you at all times. Foreigners are not exempt from the law. Seat belts are compulsory, both front and rear where fitted, and you must carry a warning breakdown triangle. Make sure that you are well supplied with screenwash and de-icer in winter as slush and mud can be a major problem on country roads. Speed limits are 60 kph in built-up areas,

90 kph on main roads and 110 kph on motorways. Do not drink and drive as the penalties for breaking the law are very severe.

By our standards the road network is very uncrowded and Czech drivers are very courteous, so you should not miss out on the lovely surroundings of Prague because you feel too nervous to drive your own or a rented car. Apart from stretches of cobbles in towns and through some villages which have been left with the express purpose of slowing up the traffic, all roads are excellent and very well maintained, even in winter. The only real drawback to the road system is that the signposting is not yet up to international standards and often signs are extremely difficult to spot, especially at night. They have white or gold letters on a blue background, but paint quality was poor and they are hard to see. That said, the motorway signs are excellent. Coming into Prague look for the signs reading 'Centrum', to take you into the city centre. See **Accidents & Breakdowns**, **Car Hire**, **Emergency Numbers**, **Parking**, **Petrol**, **Transport**.

Drugs: The use or possession of any form of narcotic substance is strictly illegal. Anyone caught smuggling drugs faces a long prison sentence with no leniency for supposed ignorance.

Dvořák, Antonín (1841-1904): Bohemia's best-known composer began life as a butcher's boy. He followed Smetana's (see **A-Z**) national trend, and he travelled widely. It was while staying in America that he composed the symphony *From the New World* which combined black spiritual themes with his native Czech folk music. He died in Prague, and is buried in the cemetery at Vyšehrad (see **A-Z**). See MUSEUMS.

Eating Out: Prague has a bewildering range of restaurants offering food ranging from top-class, four-star hotel cuisine, to the basic meat, sauerkraut and dumplings of the more popular taverns. Because of sensible planning regulations designed to preserve the historic centre, it is sometimes hard to distinguish a restaurant from the chemist next door. As well as this many of them are located either in a semi-basement of an ancient house, or at the end of a passageway into a former yard. The word to look for in Czech is *Restaurace*. One type of restaurant in

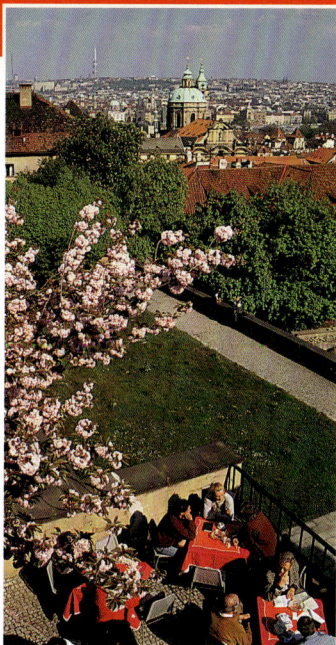

which Prague excels is the automat, of which the most famous is the Koruna (see **RESTAURANTS 3**). In these self-service eating places ready-prepared dishes are taken from behind glass flaps, and they are excellent value for money. For eating out in a more relaxed way, the list is endless. Eating houses are classified by the following titles which may help suggest both the surroundings and the food you would like: *vinárny* – usually very historic establishments where the emphasis is on the wine as well as the good choice of food; *restaurace* – more familiar straightforward restaurants; *pivnice* – pubs and taverns serving simple traditional food accompanied by beer, where there is usually a friendly if somewhat noisy atmosphere and some places may have live brass-band music; *jídelna* – these are the self-service, hot meal and snack bars in the city centre and while they are low on atmosphere, they are high on good quality, economical food; *kavárny* – the equivalent of the German and Austrian cake shop/café (*Konditorei*), with the main emphasis on leisurely coffee-drinking accompanied by high-calorie cakes and cream (small snacks such as cold meats are almost always available). As a rough guide to what you can expect to pay, a good three-course meal with either beer or Czech wine (see **Wines**) would cost around Kčs 400 plus (expensive), Kčs 150-350 (moderate) and Kčs 70-150 (inexpensive). One very important point to stress is the need to book a table at the restaurant of your choice. They are often busy all year round, but especially during the high season. Ask your hotel concierge to book for you. See **RESTAURANTS 1**, **2**, **3**, **Food**.

Electricity: 220V AC. Sockets are of the two-pinned earthed variety and visitors from the UK will need a standard adaptor. In a very few private homes in the suburbs you may find 120V in use.

Embassies:
UK – Thunovská 14, Prague 1, tel: 533347/533370.
Canada – Mickiewiczova 6, Prague 6, tel: 326941.
USA – Tržiště 15, Prague 1, tel: 536641.
At the moment, Australians, New Zealanders and other Commonwealth citizens are advised to contact the British Embassy if difficulties arise.

Emergency Numbers:

Police, inc. traffic accidents	158
Ambulance, medical assistance	155
Dentist	261374
Chemist	220081
Car breakdown	224906
Fire	150
Special intown ambulance (city centre and suburbs)	333

Events:
January: New Year is celebrated with much merrymaking.
12 May-4 June: Prague Spring Festival (*Pražské jaro*), top-quality international classical music festival.
July-August: Superb displays of folklore music, dance and stunning costumes from Bohemia, Moravia and Slovakia. Performances take place daily at 1930 on Slovanský Island by the National Theatre.
Mid-September: The concert season begins in earnest through to Christmas. Concerts are announced daily in the newspapers (see **A-Z**), or in the special ORBIS give-away booklet, *Prague – Heart of Europe*.
November: International Jazz Festival, performances are announced in the newspapers.
December: Advent and pre-Christmas festivities begin all over the city, and details of carol concerts, concerts, etc. are given in the *Prague – Heart of Europe* booklet. See **What's On**.

Food: In the days of the Austro-Hungarian Empire, Prague was considered to have some of the finest food in the realm. Under the Communist regime, because of the scarcity of many of the traditional ingredients, the culinary image became tarnished but the situation is now gradually returning to the good old days. One item, however, has remained constant and that is dumplings. Prague is without doubt, the dumpling capital of the world! *Knedlíky*, or *Knödel* in German, are light, fluffy and quite delicious. Bohemians make every conceivable variety of dumpling and they will be found on every menu, served as we would potatoes. Many dishes on menus are better recognized by their old German names (see **Language**) and menus in German will also often appear as soon as the waiter notices that you are a foreigner. For this reason both the Czech and German names for various foods are given here.

The Czech diet is largely meat based and all meats are excellent, in particular Prague ham (*Pražská šunka/Prager Schinken*), a world-famous speciality of the very highest quality. It is often the base of delicious hors d'oeuvre with stuffed tomato and whipped cottage cheese. Pragers love braised pork with dumplings and sauerkraut and you will find it on every menu, especially in the classic old Prague taverns and alehouses. The dish is called *Vepřová pečeně/Schweinebraten* and it appears with the ubiquitous *kyselé zelí*/sauerkraut in mammoth proportions. Soups are another very typical dish – *bramborová polévka/Kartoffelsuppe* is a rich mixture of beef stock, potatoes and wild mushrooms, while *hovězí polévka/Rindfleischsuppe* is a type of beef broth. Beefsteak (*biftek ruláda/Roulade*) is rolled stuffed beef, and of course there is Wiener schnitzel (*vídeňský řízek*). Hot sausages of the German variety are available at stands throughout the city. Bratwurst, a pure pork sausage, is called *klobása* in Czech, while the Frankfurter type are called *párky*. Goose (*husa/Gans*) is a speciality Sunday dish in Bohemia. If you have never tried it, do so in Prague – you will not be disappointed. Fish (*ryby/Fisch*) is excellent and the traditional Christmas dish of carp (*kapr/Karpf*) is beautifully prepared. Trout (*pstruh/Forelle*) can also be recommended. Vegetables must be asked for separately; here are a few to help you: cauliflower (*květák/Blumenkohl*); beans (*fazole/Bohnen*); potato (*brambory/Kartoffel*); tomato (*rajská jablka/Tomaten*); spinach (*špenát/Spinat*); mushrooms (*houby/Pilze* or

Champignons); peas (*hrášek/Erbsen*). The Czechs are not greatly impressed by vegetarianism and non-meat eaters may have problems trying to find vegetarian dishes.

If you have a sweet tooth, then Prague is definitely the place for you. Although desserts tend to be on the heavy side to say the least, they are delicious! *Ovocné knedlíky* are fruit-filled dumplings, stuffed with either plums (*švestky*), cherries (*třešně*) or apricots (*meruňky*). They are served in a rich butter sauce and sprinkled with icing sugar. Ice cream (*zmrzlina*) and fruit *kompot* are also delicious. Even the drabbest looking cake shop or snack bar sells the most wonderful pastries. See **RESTAURANTS 1**, **2**, **3**, **Eating Out**.

Good King Wenceslas: Duke of Bohemia (see **Bohemia**), saint, martyr and hero of the Christmas carol dedicated to him. Wenceslas (907-929) was murdered by his pagan brother Boleslav, and is buried in St. Vitus' Cathedral (see **CHURCHES 1**, **A-Z**). After his death he became the symbol of Czech nationalism, which is why Prague's main square (see **Wenceslas Square**) is named after him. Together with Agnes of Bohemia (see **St. Agnes' Convent**), Adalbert, St. John Nepomuk (see **A-Z**) and St. Vitus, he is one of the patrons of Prague.

St. Vitus' Cathedral

Health: All medical staff in Czechoslovakia are trained to a very high standard and you will be well looked after, although the surroundings leave much to be desired. Many doctors speak German and quite a few speak English as well. The Czech national health service has a reciprocal arrangement with the British health service, but emergency medical care is given free of charge to all visitors regardless of nationality. Non-British passport holders should check with their health department at home before their trip to find out if they are covered. If not, a travel insurance would certainly help. For minor ailments try the nearest chemist (see **A-Z**). For more serious problems, ask your hotel to call an English-speaking doctor. There is a special clinic for foreign visitors in central Prague at Palackého 5, off Jungmannova near Wenceslas Sq. See **Disabled People**, **Emergency Numbers**, **Insurance**.

Hus, Jan (1369-1415): A religious reformer of peasant stock, John Huss, as he is more commonly known in the West, was greatly influenced by the ideas of John Wycliffe in England. He preached in the Czech language and so became associated with the national spirit of the time. A huge statue dedicated to his memory stands in Old Town Sq. (see **WALK 1**). See **Bethlehem Chapel**.

Infant Jesus of Prague: See **WALK 3**, **Our Lady of the Victories**.

Insurance: You should take out travel insurance covering you against theft, loss of property and money, and possibly medical expenses for the duration of your stay. Your travel agent should be able to recommend a suitable policy. See **Crime & Theft**, **Driving**, **Health**.

John of Luxemburg (1296-1346): The father of Charles IV (see **A-Z**) was elected King of Bohemia (see **Bohemia**) in 1310. He died fighting on the French side against the English at the Battle of Crécy and it was from his coat of arms that Edward, The Black Prince, took the three feathers and the motto 'Ich Dien' (I serve) which the Prince of Wales bears to this day.

Josefov: The official name given to the Prague ghetto, in honour of Emperor Josef II (1780-90) who granted the Jews civil rights. The ghetto has all but gone, but the city district keeps the name. See **OLD JEWISH TOWN**.

Kafka, Franz (1883-1924): Prague born, Jewish novelist and writer who wrote in German. His works include, *The Castle*, *The Trial*, *The Judgement* and *The Hungry Artist*.

Kampa Island (Ostrov Kampa): This charming island lies on the Lesser Town (see **A-Z**) side of the Vltava river underneath Charles Bridge (see **A-Z**) and is separated from the main bank by the Čertovka channel. On it stands the Grand Prior's Water Mill (Velkopřevorský mlýn) built in 1598, as well as lovely gardens and many very attractive houses from the 17th and 18thC. See **WALK 3**.

Karlovy Vary (Karlsbad): 162 km northwest of Prague, this spa town of world renown was the glittering centre of a social whirl in the 18th and 19thC. Everyone worth their salt, including Goethe and Edward VII, came here to take the waters. You will find its elegant past lingers on in superb hotels and cafés. The waters can still be taken: contact Balnea-Cures-in-Czechoslovakia, Pařížská 11, Prague 1, or ask Čedok (see **Tourist Information**) for details. Part of your treatment should involve a swig or two of the famous *Becherovka*, invented by Dr Johann Becher in the last century, 'to improve his patients' healing' (see **Drinks**).

Karlstein Castle

Karlštejn (Karlstein) Castle: 28 km southwest of Prague. A fairytale, almost Transylvanian castle which was built in 1348-65 to house the crown jewels. The architects were the same as those who designed St. Vitus' Cathedral (see **A-Z**) – Matthias of Arras and Peter Parler (see **A-Z**). It is a favourite excursion spot for visitors. Trains run to Karlštejn every half hour from Prague main-line station (see **Railways**) and Čedok (see **Tourist Information**) arrange coach tours. See CASTLES & PALACES 2, EXCURSION 2.

Konopiště: 44 km south of Prague. The castle at Konopiště stands on a wooded hillside overlooking a lake. It was one of the favourite homes of Archduke Franz Ferdinand of Austria whose murder at Sarajevo in 1914 precipitated World War I. In his turn, he shot anything that moved and there are 300,000 trophies here to prove it! Admiral Tirpitz, Kaiser Wilhelm and members of the British royal family all came here. It now houses a magnificent collection of armour and 17th and 18thC furniture. See EXCURSION 1.

Kutná Hora (Kuttenberg): 65 km southeast of Prague. This historic silver-mining centre is also famous for its magnificent Gothic cathedral of St. Barbara and numerous quaint streets and houses. The so-called Welsh Yard (Vlašský dvůr), 'Welsh' meaning 'foreigner' here, was the place where non-German merchants met to trade in silver. In this case they were Italian and occasionally French. The magnificent Gothic building dates from 1300 and was originally constructed as a royal residence and mint. It was here that the famous international trading coin of the Middle Ages, the *groschen*, was first made with local silver. The Stone House (Kamenný dům) is a richly decorated merchant's house and is the oldest in the town. Silver mining died out in the early 1700s and Kutná Hora is now a national monument. See EXCURSION 1.

Language: The Czech language is a member of the Slavonic family and notoriously difficult for foreigners to learn. Even with a rudimentary knowledge of the pronunciation of certain letters, you will still have difficulty in saying some of the very simplest words. In spite of 40 years of obligatory teaching of Russian in the schools, by far and away the most common second tongue is German. After 900 years of continuous domination by either Germany or Austria this is not surprising and you will often find waiters, hotel staff, taxi drivers and others answering you in German. For this reason the German equivalent for various foods, drinks, etc. have been given to help you. The towns, cities and rivers of Bohemia were known to the outside world by their German names so, partly for historical reasons and partly to help the visitor with the unfamiliar Czech language, the alternative old German names have also been given where appropriate (e.g. Karlovy Vary is better known outside Czechoslovakia as Karlsbad). The next best language to try is English, which the young are very keen to learn. For the businessman in Prague however, German is a 'must'. The Slovak language spoken in the other parts of the country (see **Bohemia**) is very closely related to Czech and can be understood in the same way as an Italian would a Spaniard.

Laundries: Coin-operated Launderettes are very rare in the centre of Prague and you are best to use a laundry (*prádelna*) or a dry cleaner (*čistírna*). Costs are reasonable and service is fast and efficient, some places even providing a while-you-wait special delivery. A good, central, dry cleaner and laundry is Jitřenka, Václavské náměstí 17. Many hotels operate their own laundry service.

Lesser Town (Malá Strana): In German known as Kleinseite, meaning the Small Side, which is exactly what it was when compared to the Old Town (see **A-Z**) at its inception in the 13thC. It is now the prettiest and most complete historic area of the city, nestling under the castle (see **PRAGUE CASTLE**). See **WALK 3**.

Lidice: 25 km northwest of Prague on the road (No. 7) to Slaný. A sad reminder of the Nazis' revenge for the killing of the governor of Bohemia-Moravia, Reichsprotektor Reinhard Heydrich, in June 1942 by Czech resistance fighters (see **WALK 2**). The village's 95 houses were wiped off the map, and 173 members of the male population were shot – the oldest 84, the youngest 15. The women went to Ravensbrück concentration camp and the children to a camp in Poland. Those few who survived look after the tiny museum (0900-1700).

Lidice

Lobkowitz: The name of an ancient noble line whose several palaces adorn Prague's skyline (see CASTLES & PALACES 1). The family was immensely rich in Austro-Hungarian days and, as they were great patrons of the arts, their name occurs frequently all over the city. The present head of the house now lives in the USA. See **Our Lady of the Victories**.

Lost Property: The main lost property office is at Bolzanova 5, tel: 2368887, close to Prague main-line station (see **Railways**). It is called *Zráty a nálezy* in Czech or *Fundbüro* in German. If you have lost your passport, car papers or other documents, then go to Olšanská 2, tel: 245184, which is in the city district of Žižkov, not far from the National Monument (See **A-Z**). Tram 5 or 9 will take you straight there. Open 0830-1800. See **Insurance**.

Malé náměstí: The 'Little Square' is situated just behind the Old Town Hall (see **A-Z**). It is surrounded by lovely old houses and at the centre there sits a Renaissance fountain (1550). The architect Christoph Dientzenhofer (see **A-Z**) lived at No. 12 in 1698.

Markets: The best open-air market is around Havelská, between Rytířská and the Old Town Sq. (see **WALK 1**). There are, however, many impromptu traders in the Old Town Sq., on all the routes leading up to Prague Castle (see **A–Z**) and on Charles Bridge (see **A–Z**) selling mostly souvenirs, flowers, etc. Official markets are open 0500/0600-1200 Mon.-Sat.

Masaryk, T. G. (1886-1948): Regarded by Czechs as the Father of the Nation, he was instrumental in achieving independence from Austria in 1918. Discredited by the Communists, statues of him are now sprouting up all over the country.

Matthias of Arras (c.1290-1352): The French master builder and architect who was responsible for the design of St. Vitus' Cathedral (see **CHURCHES 1**) and Karlštejn Castle (see **EXCURSION 2**). Born in Artois, he died in Prague and is buried in St. Vitus'. His successor was Peter Parler (see **Charles Bridge**, **A–Z**).

Moldau: See **Vltava**.

Money: You are best to travel with either traveller's cheques, Deutschmark or sterling. At the present time, the Czech crown is not a convertible currency, and as such, open to all sorts of underhand exchanges on the black market. The moment you leave your hotel, or even discreetly in the lobby, you will be approached and whispered to in German 'wechsel' or 'tauschen'? – 'Do you want to change?' You are advised to change money only at your hotel, in a bank (see **Opening Times**) or in one of the numerous official exchange bureaux around the city. You may get a few crowns less, but unofficial moneychanging is illegal and you could get yourself into a lot of trouble. In any case the official rate is still very good value. There are exchange bureaux at the following places: Čedok, Na příkopě 18 (see **Tourist Information** for opening times); Chequepoint, next to Koruna Automat, at the bottom end of Václavské náměstí (0730-2100); Chequepoint, in the second courtyard of Prague Castle (0900-1800). There are many other Chequepoint branches around the city which are open every day and several mini exchange offices are being opened in and around the main tourist spots. Before you change money there, check the hotel rate first – there may be a better rate and no commission. Eurocheques will be widely accepted both for your hotel bill and to pay for goods at the duty-free Tuzex chain (see SHOPPING 1). Major credit cards are accepted everywhere. See **Crime & Theft**, **Currency**.

Mozart, Wolfgang Amadeus (1756-91): The Austrian composer visited Prague on many occasions. In 1786, after *The Marriage of Figaro* received a lukewarm reception in Vienna, he took it to Prague where it was an instant success. *Don Giovanni* was first performed in Prague in 1787 (see WALK 1) and it is thought he composed *Eine Kleine Nachtmusik* here in the same year. There is a Mozart Museum outside the city in Villa Bertramka, Mozartova 169, off the main road to Pilsen (Plzeň – see EXCURSION 3). It is open 0930-1800 daily, but it is best to check before leaving, tel: 543893; Kčs 50. See **Music**.

Municipal House (Obecní dům): Fronting náměstí Republiky (Republic Sq.) is the wonderful *Jugendstil* Municipal House, built in 1906-11. This multipurpose centre contains a restaurant (see RESTAURANTS 2), bars, a dance hall and concert facilities (see **Music Venues**), and is one of the few buildings of this style in Europe that has not succumbed to the demolition merchants or World War II bombing raids. The residence of the Bohemian kings once stood on this site (1380-1547), and from the present building, the Czechoslovakian Republic was proclaimed on 28 October, 1918.

Music: Since the time of Mozart (see **A-Z**) and Beethoven, Prague has been a major European centre for music. Many famous composers came to the city at one time or another, including Gluck, von Weber, Liszt, Wagner, Mozart, Smetana (see **A-Z**), Dvořák (see **A-Z**), Janáček, Berlioz and Tchaikovsky. The Czech Philharmonic is only one of the major international orchestras that play here on a regular basis, so that on any evening you can expect to find first-class classical entertainment at any number of venues around the city (see **Music Venues**). You could also spend a night at the opera (see **Opera & Operetta**). Organ and chamber music recitals are held almost daily in many of the splendid churches and monasteries dotted around Prague – hearing Vivaldi, live, in a baroque church is an unforgettable experience. If you want something a bit more lively, there are dozens of discos and rock venues as well as many jazz clubs. There is plenty of brass-band music to be heard in the city's beer halls as well as traditional folklore concerts with both music and dancing (see **Events**). If you are visiting in summer, do not forget to enquire at your hotel about the open-air concerts which are held in the magnificent gardens of Prague's palaces and castles (see **CASTLES & PALACES 1 & 2**). See **What's On**.

Music Venues: There are concert halls for all types of music, although the majority are for classical. The main ones are: The Smetana Hall, Obecní dům, náměstí Republiky 5, tel: 2325858 (performances at 1900 daily; 1400 Sat., Sun.; Metro Náměstí Republiky; tram 5, 14, 26); the National Theatre, Národní (performances as for the Smetana Hall; tram 9, 17, 18, 21, 22); the Karlin Theatre of Music & Operetta, Křižíkova 10, tel: 220895 (Metro Florenc; tram 3, 8, 24); the Palace of Culture, 5 května 65, tel: 4172741 (Metro Vyšehrad); the Spanish Hall, inside the Prague Castle complex (no telephone booking, ask at your hotel for details; access best by taxi). Rock concerts usually take place at the Palace of Culture (see above) and are well advertised in the press and by posters. Jazz fans should try the Press Jazz Club, 2nd floor, Pařížská 9, (2100-0200 Mon.-Sat.; entry Kčs 30). See press and posters for the programme. Admittance charges to all cultural events are ridiculously low compared to Western prices. See **Music**, **Opera & Operetta**, **What's On**.

Na příkopě: Prague's main shopping street is built on the remains of a filled-in moat (the name in Czech means 'At the Moat'). The rubble came from the town walls, and the work was completed in 1781. It is located between the Old and New Towns (see **A-Z**). See **WALKS 1 & 2**.

National Monument (Národní památník): The massive National Monument stands in a hilly park area known as Vítkov (see **PARKS & GARDENS**). It is easily located at the far end of Hybernská where it joins Husitská. Built 1926-1938, it houses the tomb of the unknown warrior and other national notables. However, what most foreigners come to see is the huge equestrian statue of Jan Žižka, the medieval Czech hero, which stands at over 9 m high. It is the largest statue of its kind in the world. The park is also an excellent place for picnics.

National Museum (Národní muzeum): Standing at the top of Wenceslas Square (see **A-Z**), this imposing structure dates from 1890. The view down the square from the terrace is superb. It contains exhibits dating from prehistoric times to the 1940s including objects from the interwar period, a coin collection and a natural history section. However, as all the labelling is in Czech, the displays may not be of very much interest. It also has an excellent, quiet, snack bar. The museum is open 0900-1600 Mon., Fri.; 0900-1700 Wed., Thu., Sat., Sun; Kčs 10. Metro Muzeum; tram 11.

Nepomuk, St. John (c.1350-80): Patron saint of Bohemia (see **A-Z**) who was drowned in the Vltava river when he was thrown from Charles Bridge for opposing King Wenceslas IV. St. Vitus' Cathedral (see **A-Z**) contains his massive silver tomb. See CHURCHES 2.

Newspapers: After 40 years of the Communist *Morning Star*, mainstream English-language newspapers are slowing finding their way back onto the streets and into the hotels of Prague. You will find the *Guardian International* widely available, together with the *European*, *Herald Tribune*, *Time* magazine and the *Financial Times*. There is no local English-language paper, but the weekly *Neue Prager Presse* can prove useful even if you cannot read German as it contains a 'what's on' for the theatre, cinema and music scene and is available free from Čedok offices (see **Tourist Information**). See **What's On**.

New Town (Nové Město): This part of the city was laid out by Charles IV (see **A-Z**) in the 1340s to expand the town outside the walls and moat. It is a most attractive area, and the broad uncluttered streets are a complete contrast to the narrow winding lanes of the Old Town (see **A-Z**) and the hilly Lesser Town (see **A-Z**). There are two immense 'squares' – Wenceslas (see **A-Z**) and Charles – actually more oblong in shape. The 80,000 sq. m Charles Sq. (Karlovo náměstí) was intended for royal tournaments and other outdoor events as well as for displays of loyalty to the crown. The crown jewels were also displayed here. Most of the buildings here today date from the 18th and 19thC, apart from the New Town Hall which was built in the 14thC. See WALK 2.

Nightlife: Although Prague is not in the same league as many other European cities when it comes to nightlife, there is plenty for visitors of all age groups and tastes to do. If you like the good old-fashioned pub-type atmosphere then try one of the traditional Prague taverns (see RESTAURANTS 2 & 3) or for a more sedate evening, listen to the Palm Court Quartet playing in the Europa Hotel café (see CAFÉS). For the young at heart there are plenty of very lively discos in and around Wenceslas Square (see A–Z). Despite the proliferation of signs, the entrances will not always be easily spotted from the main street as they are nearly all in passageways and shopping arcades off the square. There are also plenty of clubs with shows, but note that as many of these are popular it is advisable to book (your hotel porter will be able to help). For those who like the peaceful classical atmosphere, Prague is the ideal place to be, with concerts and recitals going on all over the city. Ask Prague Information Service, Čedok (see **Tourist Information**) and at your hotel for all the latest information on the nightlife scene. See NIGHTLIFE, **Music**, **Music Venues**, **Opera & Operetta**.

St. Nicholas' Church

Old Town (Staré Město): This part of the city has its origins back in the 12thC when it grew up around the marketplace (Staroměstské náměstí). Merchants from as far away as Samarkand came here to trade, and the city centre grew up around it. The historic square (see **MUSTS**) is still the focal point of the Old Town and contains the Old Town Hall (see **A-Z**), Astronomical Clock (see **A-Z**), churches, a palace and many other lovely old buildings. See **WALK 1**.

Old Town Hall (Staroměstská radnice): Located in the Old Town Square (Staroměstské náměstí), this was the seat of administration of the Old Town district. It was completed with its tower in 1364, and what you see today are only parts of the original structure which was 'restored' in the 19thC and unfortunately burnt down at the end of World War II. See **WALK 1**, **Astronomical Clock**.

Opening Times: Prague's opening hours are unusually long compared to those in other European cities. It is not unusual for example to find food shops open at 0600 and still going at 1800. In general:
Shops – 0800/0830-1200, 1300/1400-1900 Mon.-Fri. (department stores are open through lunch), 0800/0830-1300 Sat. (in many tourist areas open all day Sat.).
Banks – 0800-1200, 1300-1700 Mon.-Fri. Bureaux de change are open until at least 2200.
Museums – 0900/1000-1700/1800 Tue.-Sun. (unless otherwise stated).
Post Offices – 0830-1800 Mon.-Fri.

Opera & Operetta: Most of the more popular, as well as some of the rather obscure operas are produced regularly in Prague, and at prices that anyone can afford. Lavish productions take place not only at the National and Smetana theatres, but also at several other venues throughout the capital (see **Music Venues**). To find out what is on check with your hotel, look for posters around the city and ask Prague Information Service (see **Tourist Information**) for the latest details.

Normally, it is not a problem to get tickets. However, when all the big names arrive for the Prague Spring Festival (see **Events**), and opera lovers from Vienna and Berlin to see them, the situation becomes more difficult. Old traditions die hard in Prague, and there are shades of the Austro-Hungarian days still around when it comes to the operetta scene. You can see excellent productions of all the old favourites like the *Merry Widow*, *Countess Maritza*, and of course *Rose-Marie*. See **Theatre Ticket Service**, **What's On**.

Orientation: It is not as easy to find your way around Prague as it is some cities because of the large number of ancient, twisting streets and alleys whose layout has hardly altered in centuries. The Vltava (Moldau) river runs through the centre of the city with the Old and New Towns on the east side and the Lesser Town and castle district (Hradčany) to the west. The Old and New Towns are roughly separated by Na příkopě (the main shopping street) and Národní (one of the main thorough-fares), with the Old Town Sq. (Staroměstské náměstí) and Wenceslas Sq. (Václavské náměstí) their respective centres. If you get lost near the river, keep an eye on Prague Castle and the lookout tower in Petřín park to bring you back to the Charles Bridge. It is worth remembering the names in Czech of streets, squares, etc., to help you find your hotel again: *náměstí* (square); *ulice* (street); *třída* (avenue); *most* (bridge); Vltava (River Moldau). You may also be confronted by two number-plates on some of the buildings. The blue plaque indicates the normal street number, while the red one is historical, the number here indicating the order in which buildings were noted in the land register, so that the lower the number, the older the building.

Our Lady of Loreto (Loreta): The Loreto Church and monastery were built in 1626-31, with the facade finished later by the Dientzenhofers (see **A-Z**) in 1722. It contains a copy of the so-called Holy House of Loreto, said to have been the house of Jesus' family, which was flown to Italy by angels in 1294. (Our Lady of Loreto is the patron of aviators!) The church also has a magnificent treasury (Loretánský klášter) and a famous carillon, made in Holland in 1694, which sounds every hour. See **CHURCHES 1**, **MUSTS**, **PRAGUE CASTLE**.

Our Lady of the Victories (kostel Panny Marie Vítězné):
Construction began on this, the earliest baroque building in Prague, in
1611. The former Carmelite church contains the famous statue of the
Infant Jesus of Prague. This statuette is an object of veneration for mil-
lions of people from around the world. It was made near Córdoba in
Spain by a monk who had a vision of the Christchild, and the figure
came to Prague when a Spanish noblewoman married a member of the
Lobkowitz family (see **A-Z**). It has been in this church since 1628. In
summer, busloads of the faithful arrive (especially from Latin America
and the Philippines) to see the minute figure in its red cloak and crown.
See **WALK 3**.

Parking: As much of the Old Town and the Wenceslas Sq. area is
pedestrianized, the best plan if exploring this part of the city, would be to
leave your car parked in the special spaces allocated to your hotel. You
will be given a blue-and-white card with the word *Réservé* on it in large
letters, and the number of your vehicle. Without this permit you could be
towed away (with tow-away costs starting at Kčs 500). Although traffic is
light by our standards, parking fines are not. Several department stores
have underground car parks and costs are minimal. Parking meters are
in use in some business districts, notably around Wenceslas Sq.;
charges are Kčs 5 for 2 hr. Parking is easier in the upper part of the
Lesser Town, near the Loreto Church (see **CHURCHES 1**, **Our Lady of
Loreto**), from where you can walk to Prague Castle and down to the
Lesser Town sights. See **Car Hire**, **Driving**.

Parler, Peter (1330-99): A German architect (originally from Swäbisch
Gmünd) who came to Prague to continue the work on St. Vitus'
Cathedral (see **CHURCHES 1**, **A-Z**) after the death of Matthias of Arras
(see **A-Z**). His most famous work, however, is the Charles Bridge (see
A-Z). His curious surname comes from *parlier*, the old French for 'fore-
man', perhaps from early contacts in France through his father who was
also a talented mason.

Passports & Customs: British passport holders no longer need a visa
to enter Czechoslovakia but a full passport is recommended rather than

a British visitor's passport. Most Commonwealth citizens, including Australians and New Zealanders, still need a visa. Check first before leaving home. Until recently, it was necessary to register with the police after a stay of more than five days in private households. This is now being abolished for non-visa visitors, but do check with the Czechoslovakian Embassy in your own country before you set out as to whether this is still the case for your particular non-British passport. The USA has its own arrangements which are under review at present. See **Customs Allowances**, **Embassies**.

Petrol: There are plenty of filling stations in Czechoslovakia, the network is called Benzina. Petrol is available as Normal and Special (not recommended for most Western cars), Super (96 octane) and lead-free (91 octane), the latter becoming more readily available as visitors come into the country. You will usually see the sign for lead-free petrol written in German – *Bleifrei* (the Czech word is *natural*). In the city there is a 24-hr station at Argentinská, over Hlávkův Bridge. There is also a 24-hr station called Motol on the Plzeň motorway at the city boundary. Filling stations are usually open 0600-2000. See **Driving**.

Place Names: See **Language**.

Plzeň (Pilsen): 90 km southwest of Prague, Pilsen is Bohemia's (see **A-Z**) second city, and although very industrial it has a great deal of interest for visitors besides the famous brewery (see **Drinks**). There is the lovely church of St. Bartholomew situated in the large market square, a superb Town Hall (1556), a good Brewery Museum, numerous little streets to explore, as well as plenty of interest in the surrounding countryside. Pilsen is also home to the huge Škoda armaments works, in a tradition that goes back to the Middle Ages when armour was made here. See **EXCURSION 3**.

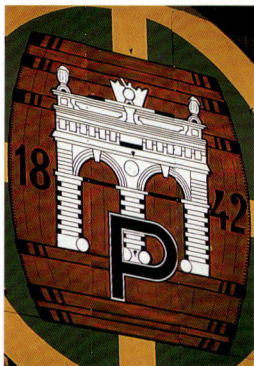

Police: Czechoslovakian police (*Policie* in Czech) are very helpful and many speak a number of languages including English, especially those on duty in the main tourist areas. The police uniforms are a greyish or dark-green colour, with green trimmings on the epaulettes and caps. There are police stations in every city district of Prague, with the headquarters (open 24 hr) in the aptly named Konviktská street, in the Old Town (see **A-Z**), between Betlémské náměstí and the river (see **Vltava**). In an emergency, tel: 158. Emergency telephones can be found in many streets and at Metro stations. See **Crime & Theft**, **Emergency Numbers**.

Post Offices: In general, post offices are open 0830-1800 Mon.-Fri., but the main office at Jindřišská 14, not far from where it crosses Wenceslas Sq., is open 24 hr. Telephone, postal and telegraph services are available at the main office. There is also a poste restante service here, but you must take your passport to collect mail. Letters and cards sent within Europe take two to five days for delivery, while mail for further afield (Australia, USA, etc.) takes much longer, sometimes up to ten days. Postcards cost Kčs 4.50 for Europe, and letters up to 20 g, Kčs 5. Make sure you ask for airmail if sending to overseas destinations – it is best to use the German word *Luftpost* which will be understood. You can also buy stamps in Tabak shops (see **Smoking**). Czech stamps have always been collectors' favourites – try to get something unusual on your cards. Letter boxes are an orange-yellow colour. See **Telephones & Telegrams**.

Powder Tower (Prašná brána): This is the only remaining city gate in Prague dating from the Middle Ages. Built in 1475, the Powder Tower once stood guard over the city wall, which at this point was next to the old royal town residence now replaced by the Municipal House (see **A-Z**) in Republic Sq. In the 18thC the tower was used as a gunpowder store, hence its name. It marks the beginning of the old 'Royal Path' which led down Celetná, across Charles Bridge and up to St. Vitus' Cathedral where the coronations took place (see **WALK 1**). It is possible to climb to the top of the 65 m-high tower (1000-1700 April-Oct.; Kčs 5). Metro Náměstí Republiky; tram 5, 14, 26.

Prague Castle (Pražský hrad): A stronghold for centuries, Prague Castle was first fortified in the 9thC and building continued right up to 1929 when St. Vitus' Cathedral (see **A-Z**), which is within the castle precincts, was completed. The castle covers the whole hilltop above the Lesser Town (see **A-Z**) and is a huge complex of palaces, gardens, churches, parks, convents and a monastery all in one which can be seen from all over the city. It looks particulary splendid at night when it is floodlit. It is extremely interesting but it does take a very long time to explore so it is suggested that you treat it as a full-day excursion. See **ART GALLERIES, CASTLES & PALACES 1, CHURCHES 1, MUSTS, PARKS & GARDENS, PRAGUE CASTLE**.

Přemysl: This was the earliest royal dynasty of Bohemia (see **A-Z**) which began when a semi-legendary peasant, Přemysl, married the Bohemian princess Libussa in the 8thC, giving his name to the line (see **Vyšehrad**). Their successors united Bohemia into one duchy and completed the Christianizing of the land. The most famous member of the family was Wenceslas (see **Good King Wenceslas**).

Public Holidays: 1 Jan.; Easter Mon. (Velikonoční pondělí); 1 May (May Day – Svátek práce); 8 May (commemorates end of World War II in Europe); 5 July (Day of Constantine and Methodius); 6 July (Day of Jan Hus – see **Hus**); 28 Oct. (Day of Independent Czechoslovakia, 1918); 24-26 Dec.; (Christmas Eve, Christmas Day, St. Stephen's Day).

Railways: Czechoslovakia has a very dense and efficient rail network. At very low cost you could visit Karlovy Vary (see **A-Z**) for the day, or travel even further afield without having to worry about driving. If you plan to use the fast through trains called *Expresní* or *Rychlik*, you will need reservations for seats. Prague's main-line railway station (Praha hlavní nádraží) is located on Wilsonova, not far from the National Museum (see **A-Z**). The station building is a protected monument because of its exuberant and very unusual *Jugendstil* architecture. Ask Čedok for details, or ask at the main station about route maps, times, etc. For enquiries, tel: 264930, although you may have language difficulties. If so, ask your hotel reception to help out. See **Transport**.

Religious Services: Prague is a predominantly Roman Catholic city and Masses are said every day in all the main places of worship. Unfortunately, it is rare to find services in foreign languages although this is likely to change with the influx of visitors from around the world. Very occasionally, Masses are said in French and German (on Sun. only) at kostel Panny Marie Vítězné which houses the famous infantile statue (see **Our Lady of the Victories**). Protestant services are hard to come by in spite of the large number of reformed churches. Enquire at the British or American embassies whether they know of any service (see **Embassies**). Jewish visitors can worship at the Old-New Synagogue (see OLD JEWISH TOWN) and details of times are available from the Chief Rabbi's office in the Jewish Town Hall next door. Muslims and other groups are not well provided for. See CHURCHES 1 & 2.

Rudolf II (1552-1612): Holy Roman Emperor and King of Bohemia (see **A-Z**). In spite of embarking on some disastrous wars, plus fits of melancholy and even madness, he put together one of the finest art collections Europe had ever seen. The remnants of it can be seen in the Picture Gallery at Prague Castle (see **A-Z**) and elsewhere in the city. See ART GALLERIES.

St. Agnes' Convent (Anežský klášter): Founded in 1234 by Agnes of Bohemia, a favourite patron of Prague who was canonized in 1989. It now forms a part of the National Gallery (see ART GALLERIES) and contains a collection of Czech 19th and 20thC paintings as well as an interesting collection of 19thC handicrafts (1000-1700 Tue.-Sun.).

St. Nicholas' Church (Chrám svatého Mikuláše): Located in the Lesser Town (see **A-Z**), this church is not to be confused with the one of the same name (see CHURCHES 2) in the Old Town Sq. It contains magnificent ceiling frescoes and the massive statues of the saints under the dome are the largest in Prague. See CHURCHES 1, WALK 3.

St. Vitus' Cathedral (svatý Vít): A superb Gothic structure within the Prague Castle complex. Located on an ancient site, the present building was begun in 1344 by Matthias of Arras (see **A-Z**) and Peter Parler (see **A-Z**) but was not finally completed until 1929. Among its many treasures, it houses the tomb of St. Wenceslas (see **Good King Wenceslas**) in a splendid chapel decorated with semiprecious stones. See **CHURCHES 1**, **PRAGUE CASTLE**.

Shopping: While Prague is not renowned for its shopping, there are a lot of bargains for the keen-eyed shopper to pick up. Apart from Na příkopě and the Wenceslas Sq. districts, you can pass a happy hour or two wandering along Celetná and Karlova streets in the Old Town, window-shopping and admiring the ancient buildings as you go. The department stores, although nothing special, do have a good selection of bargains which make excellent gifts, like handicrafts and table linen. The duty-free range of Tuzex (see **SHOPPING 1**), while not that cheap, certainly beats any airport shop on price. See **SHOPPING 1 & 2**, **Best Buys**, **Markets**, **Opening Times**.

Smetana, Bedřich (1824-84): The Czech composer was the first to create a 'national' style of music, which owed much to Slav folk themes and was the antithesis of the formal Austro-Hungarian music popular in Vienna at this time. It stirred Czech audiences to show their national spirit after centuries of Austrian rule. An example of this type of national music is *Má Vlast* (*My Fatherland*), a symphonic poem about Bohemia. Smetana died in Prague and is buried in Vyšehrad cemetery.

Smoking: Prague has an unusual unwritten law that in many restaurants and snack bars, no smoking is allowed between 1000-1400. This does not apply to the beer halls. Smoking is not permitted in shops or on public transport. However, there are smoking compartments on long-distance trains. Tobacconist shops in Prague are called Tabák.

Sports: For a small nation, Czechoslovakia has produced more than its fair share of sportsmen and women over the last 50 years. This is particularly true for tennis and athletics. The facilities in Prague are excellent and better than you would expect to find in a city twice its size. There are five major sports halls, 13 stadiums, six winter-sports centres, eight indoor pools and 13 open-air baths. Added to this, there are three complete tennis complexes, a golf club (on the Plzeň road at Motol, Prague 5, tel: 521098), horse racing and bowling facilities, and virtually every city district also has a large sauna centre.
In order to take full advantage of the facilities on offer, contact Sport-Turist, Národní 33, tel: 263351 (0900-1800 Mon.-Fri., 0900-1200 Sat.) where they will provide you, free of charge, with a list giving details of all sports facilities, opening times and charges. The quality of Czech sports articles is so good, you may wish to purchase instead. In that case go to Dům Sportu (House of Sport), literally round the corner at Jungmannova 28 (see **SHOPPING 2**). Even if you do not wish to participate, you may be interested to visit the Tennis Centre on Štvanice Island (Ostrov Štvanice) which is crossed by the Hlávkův Bridge. You can watch budding stars practising and you can even play here, but you must book a court in advance, tel: 2311270 (Metro Florenc; tram 3, 8,).

Strahov Monastery (Strahovský klášter): Founded on the heights above the Lesser Town (see **A-Z**) in 1148, the present building dates from the end of the 18thC. It contains a magnificent library (1679) which has a fabulous collection of books, manuscripts and maps. The library also has the most amazing ceiling frescoes, added in 1727. It is open 0930-1130, 1300-1630 Tue.-Sun.; Kčs 20 for the museum and library. See **PRAGUE CASTLE**.

Library, Strahov Monastery

Students: Students are very well catered for in Prague and everything is done to help them enjoy their visit at the lowest possible cost. The CKM (Youth Travel Bureau), Žitná 10, Prague 1, deals exclusively with cheap student accommodation across the city. They are open 0700-1900 (or later) Mon.-Sat. in summer, 0900-1800 Mon.-Fri. in winter. (If you arrive on a Sun. and need accommodation, you could try the Junior Hotel next door at Žitná 12.) CKM can arrange accommodation at hostels across Prague for Kčs 120-250 per night. No advance booking is necessary and you do not need an IYHF card, however, cardholders can get discount in July and August. CKM will also answer any questions on touring the rest of the country.

Student travellers can now get a reduction on international rail tickets into and out of Czechoslovakia on production of an International Student Identity Card (ISIC) and a passport (not a British visitor's passport). They also have access to all Prague's museums and theatres at a fraction of the normal cost as well as reduced rates on the Metro and trams (see **Transport**). Note that none of the Čedok offices (see **Tourist Information**) deal with student accommodation.

Taxis: Taxis are both cheap and easy to find, and all carry the sign 'Taxi' on the roof. All models of car are used, including the impressive Tatra and Moskvitch, although the most popular is the home-produced workhorse, the Škoda. The most accessible ranks in the city centre are in Wenceslas Sq. by the Hvězda cinema, and in the Old Town Sq. at the corner of Pařížská. Most taxi drivers can understand German; English is something of a rarity. It would be best to write down on a piece of paper the name of your destination in Czech to show to the driver. Don't forget to give the driver a 10% tip (see **Tipping**). Your hotel should be able to help you with booking taxis.

Telephones & Telegrams: Telephone kiosks can be found all over the city, but only a few newly-installed phonecard machines (there is one at Metro Muzeum) will handle international calls. You are advised to go to the main post office (see **Post Office**) or make the call from your hotel room (more expensive). To book an international call, dial 0139 and ask the operator to put you through. To make enquiries, tel: 0149. Local calls from a pay phone cost Kčs 1, for which you will need the appropriate coin (see **Currency**). Reverse-charge/collect calls can pose problems. Telegrams can be sent from all post offices, both cheaply and easily. Simply fill in the form and hand it back to the clerk. Ask for a 'telegram'.

Television & Radio: Unless you are a Czech speaker, most of the radio and television programmes will not be of much interest to you. That said, there is a new TV channel called OK 3 which broadcasts 24-hr programmes such as the American CNN news, and a variety of entertainment in English, German and French. The BBC 9 o'clock news is also broadcast on Czech TV around 2400 daily. Prague is just a bit too far from the border with either Austria or Germany to pick up TV signals. On the radio there is a tourist service broadcast in English, German and French on the short-wave band from 0600-1200 (kHz 6055/45.55 m; kHz 7345/40.85 m; kHz 9505/31.56 m). There is also a new private service called *Hello World* on 93.7 FM from 0900-1200.

Theatre Ticket Service: Advance tickets can be bought at the special kiosk in the ALFA-cinema passage off Wenceslas Sq. (0830-1900). It is worth checking with your hotel concierge first, as he/she may have spare tickets for a popular show. Beware of ticket touts for big-name concerts – you can be fleeced. See **Music Venues**, **Opera & Operetta**.

Time Difference: Czechoslovakia is 1 hr ahead of GMT. The clocks go forward in the summer making it 1 hr ahead of BST.

Tipping: In general tips are included in the bill. However, a small gratuity is always welcome for good or friendly service. Taxi drivers expect 10% while hotel porters, chambermaids, etc. will accept what is given. Cloakroom and toilet attendants should be given Kčs 1-5.

Toilets: There are public toilets in the ticket halls of all Metro stations and they are clean and cost Kčs 1-2. There are also toilets at many of the tourist sights around the city. Do not be worried about using the facilities of a café or restaurant even if you are not a customer – it is quite the accepted thing in Prague. Ladies is *Ženy* or *Dámy* and the gents *Muži* or *Páni*. Sometimes you see it written in German as well; *Damen* and *Herren* respectively. See **Tipping**.

Tourist Information: Čedok has been looking after the tourists' needs in Czechoslovakia for well over 70 years. Once a private company, it was nationalized under the Communist regime, and is now set to be privatized again. It is in the strange position of being a tour operator and national tourist board in one. As such they are experts in Czech travel and you can call at the main office in Na příkopě 18, tel: 2127111 for all information (0830-1900). You can also try Prague Information Service, Na příkopě 20, tel: 544444, practically next door, (0800-2030 Mon.-Fri., till 2200 June-Sep.; 0900-1500 Sat., Sun.). Pragotur, U Obecního domu, will also arrange accommodation and tours (0800-2030 Mon.-Fri., 1000-1800 Sat., 1000-1500 Sun.). In the Old Town, at Malé náměstí 14, is the American Hospitality Center-Prague, tel: 2367486, a non-profit-making organization to help young people find their way around. Curiously, it seems more popular with young German, British and Australian visitors than the Americans themselves! If you want advance information before your trip, contact Čedok at 17-18 Old Bond St, London, W1X 3DA, tel: 071-6296058/9. Elsewhere contact your local Czech embassy and ask for details. Čedok will be able to supply you with a tailor-made holiday to suit your needs. Ask them to send you a brochure giving all their services and tours. Even if travelling independently it is advisable to book your hotel through Čedok. See **Accommodation**, **Tours**, **What's On**.

Tours: Tours in Prague are run by Čedok or Pragotur (see **Tourist Information**) or by a number of newly-established private agencies. They can offer city sightseeing tours, trips on the river (see **Boat Trips**) and further afield to the castles and historic sights around Prague, as well as a 'Prague by Night' tour with visits to cabarets, beer halls, etc.

Transport: Prague has an excellent public transport system with trams, Metro and buses fully integrated. There are three underground lines, all of which connect with the tramway and bus routes. In general, trams run in the inner city, while buses cope with the outer suburbs. Tickets, valid for one trip only, are available from yellow vending machines at station booking offices, at newsagents and the Tabak shops (see **Smoking**), as well as some hotels. You will need a ticket for large pieces of luggage; children under 10 years of age travel free. You must validate your ticket by punching it in the machine before you go onto the Metro platform (watch other passengers) or as you enter the tram or bus. Tickets cost Kčs 4 and they can not be used to transfer from one form of transport to another – you will need to buy separate tickets for each leg of your journey (although you can change from one line to the other on the Metro). If you want to avoid this problem, travel cards are a good idea. They cover periods of two to seven days and cost Kčs 15-40 depending on the number of days valid. These tickets are ideal for exploring the city and an added bonus is that you can use the ticket on the funicular railway up to Petřín park (see PARKS & GARDENS, WALK 3). Tickets are available at all travel agents such as Čedok (see **Tourist Information**), at many hotel receptions and from the headquarters of Prague Municipal Transport Authority at Na Bojišti 5. Do not try to travel without a ticket as you could be fined Kčs 100, as well as having to pay for an extra ticket and go through endless formalities with the inspector. The Metro runs 0500-2400, trams run 24 hr (but at long intervals during the night) and buses run, in general, from 0500-2400 with most night services every 40 min to the outlying suburbs. See **Railways**.

Vltava River & Lakes

Traveller's Cheques: See **Money**.

Vltava (Moldau): Prague's river rises in the Bohemian Forest close to the German border, and flows northwestwards via the brewing town of České Budějovice (Budweis), and the Slapy dams (see **EXCURSION 1**) to Prague. At Mělník it joins the Elbe-Labe river in a spectacular watersmeet under the shadow of the castle and vineyard terraces. The Vltava is 430 km in length, and connects Prague to the port of Hamburg, as well as a network of inland waterways. See **Boat Trips**.

Vyšehrad: On a high bluff above the Vltava (see **A-Z**), this site was the first to be fortified by the Přemysl line (see **A-Z**), and it was here that the legendary princess Libussa supposedly founded Prague. For this reason it has great national and religious meaning for the Czechs. Many national heroes are buried in the Vyšehrad cemetery and you will find the graves of Dvořák (see **A-Z**) and Smetana (see **A-Z**) among others. Also on the Vyšehrad site is the chapel of St. Martin (see **CHURCHES 2**), and in the Karlach park stands an ancient, possibly prehistoric monument of three tubular granite shapes. They form a tripod and their purpose and origin are unknown. Metro Vyšehrad; tram 7, 18, 24.

Wenceslas Square (Václavské náměstí): More of a rectangle than a square, it was first laid out in 1348 by Charles IV (see **A-Z**) and known as the Horse Market. Now the centre of modern Prague, it is surrounded by buildings of many periods, but chiefly 19th and 20thC styles. It has always been the gathering place in which the citizens of Prague have given vent to their feelings, and was the scene of some very harrowing incidents during the Prague Spring demonstrations in 1968 against the Soviet invaders. When speaking to tourists Czechs will often refer to it by its old German name of 'Wenzelsplatz'. See **WALK 2**.

What's On: Prague does not have a complete 'what's on' guide at the moment. However, there is a most useful English-language publication edited by ORBIS, Vinohradská 46, Prague 2, which carries some very handy tips on what to see and do. The booklet is called *Prague – Heart of Europe* and appears monthly. It has a theatre and concert guide for the month ahead and will also give you details of special exhibitions at galleries and museums around the city, although it does not tell you how to get there. It is distributed free at all hotels and information centres. Otherwise, look out for posters, handbills, etc. which you will find in great profusion around the city. See **Events**, **Newspapers**.

Wines: Although practically unknown outside their native land, Czechoslovakia produces some good German-type wines which can be enjoyed at the *vinárny* (wine) bars all over Prague (see **Eating Out**). Ruhlander is the most popular and comes either red (*červené*) or white (*bílé*). They are inexpensive and very drinkable.

Youth Hostels: See **Students**.

Zoological Gardens (Zoologická zahrada): Prague's zoo is one of the world's most prestigious, and is located in delightful wooded surroundings in the suburb of Troja right next to the famous palace of the same name (see CASTLES & PALACES 2). It can be reached by a special shuttle-bus service (No. 112) which runs from the forecourt of the Metro station at Nádraží Holešovice direct to the zoo entrance. The journey time is barely 20 min in all, from the centre. See CHILDREN.

This book was produced using QuarkXPress™
and Adobe Illustrator 88™ on Apple
Macintosh™ computers and output to separated
film on a Linotronic™ 300 Imagesetter

Text: John Walker
Photography: Neil Emmerson
Electronic Cartography: Susan Harvey Design

First published 1992
Copyright © HarperCollins Publishers
Published HarperCollins Publishers
Printed in Hong Kong
ISBN 0 00 435907 0

**Guidebook information is subject to being
outdated by changes to opening hours,
prices, and by fluctuating restaurant
standards. Every effort has been made to
give you an up-to-date text but the
publishers cannot accept any liability for
errors, omissions or changes in detail or for
any consequences arising from the use of
information contained herein.
The publishers welcome corrections and
suggestions from readers; write to:
The Publishing Manager, Travel Guides,
HarperCollins Publishers, PO Box,
Glasgow G4 ONB.**